United America

The surprising truth about American
values, American identity and the
10 beliefs that a large majority
of Americans hold dear

Wayne Baker

Read The Spirit Books
an imprint of
David Crumm Media, LLC
Canton, Michigan

For more information and further discussion, visit

www.UnitedAmericaBook.com

Cover art and design by
Rick Nease
www.RickNeaseArt.com

Published By
Read The Spirit Books
an imprint of
David Crumm Media, LLC
42015 Ford Rd., Suite 234
Canton, Michigan, USA

For information about customized editions, bulk purchases
or permissions, contact David Crumm Media, LLC at info@
DavidCrummMedia.com

Contents

Dedication

TO MY DEAR son, Harrison Steele Baker.

UNITED AMERICA

America's Ten Core Values

Wayne Baker

1. **Respect for others:** Acceptance and appreciation of people of different racial, ethnic and religious groups
2. **Symbolic patriotism:** An emotional connection to country; feeling good when seeing the American flag or hearing the national anthem
3. **Freedom:** Having the right to participate in politics and elections; expression of unpopular ideas without fearing for one's safety
4. **Security:** Keeping the nation safe and secure from external and internal threats
5. **Self-reliance & individualism:** Reliance on oneself; independence; emphasis on individual strengths and accomplishments
6. **Equal opportunity:** Equal access to jobs, education, voting, etc. regardless of age, gender, race, or other factors; a level playing field
7. **Getting ahead:** Individual achievement, status, and success
8. **Pursuit of happiness:** Enjoyment, leisure, pleasure
9. **Justice & fairness:** All the world's people should live in harmony; justice and fairness for all, even people we don't know
10. **Critical patriotism:** Tough love of country; criticism of America stems from love of country and desire for improvement

About the Research

This book is unique. It's different from the many manifestos published by political activists, because UNITED AMERICA is based on years of scientific research at one of the nation's leading universities. Dr. Wayne Baker's finding that ten core values unite the vast majority of Americans is a startling conclusion, drawn from rigorous nationwide research. These ten core values were identified from data collected in four nationally representative surveys administered over a two-year period by the University of Michigan Institute for Social Research (ISR), the world's premier survey research organization. The surveys were funded in part by the ISR and the Carnegie Corporation of New York. Dr. Baker and his team designed their survey questionnaire after in-depth analysis of past research methods followed by extensive pre-survey research with focus groups, cognitive interviews, and pilot tests. The data were analyzed with a battery of statistical techniques to ensure the validity and reliability of the results.

Contact Dr. Baker

Dr. Baker is available for interviews, talks, keynote addresses, and seminars. Contact him at OurValuesProject@gmail.com.

Additional Resources

Visit www.UnitedAmericaBook.com for free downloadable discussion guides, video clips, links, and other resources for individual and group use.

Join our ongoing conversation about values and ethics in America at www.OurValues.org, a blog devoted to civil discussion of tough issues in contemporary American society. Founded in 2008, OurValues.org covers a wide range of topics and draws readers from around the world.

This book also is uniquely flexible for use with your organization or event. Group orders of this book can be modified to add your group's logo and additional pages welcoming your readers. For more information on this unusual option, visit www.UnitedAmericaBook.com.

Endorsement by
James S. Jackson

UNITED AMERICA **DOES** a tremendous service not only to the social sciences but also to the American public. We have been struggling over the last decade or so, being told about the divisiveness that pervades America, especially in American politics. This timely book documents in great detail that there are ten core values that unite us all across race, ethnicity, gender, social class and even political orientation. This is a book that brings a hopeful message and urges us all to pay attention to the core beliefs that undergird the American ethos and bind us all together."

—*James S. Jackson, Director and Research Professor, University of Michigan Institute for Social Research, and Daniel Katz Distinguished University Professor of Psychology.*

Preface by
Brian D. McLaren

WHILE I WAS reading Dr. Wayne Baker's important and uplifting new book, a strangely disturbing sentence from another book, the author and title of which are long forgotten, snuck back into my memory.

I came across that chilling sentence back in the 1990's, when I was first exploring the discipline of systems thinking. It went something like this: If you want to destroy a bridge or building, you have to detonate several explosives in several places simultaneously; otherwise, the one part of the structure that has been weakened will be propped up by the others that remain strong.

I don't think many would write such a sentence in the years since September 11, 2001, when this kind of abstract architectural principle was tragically manifested in space and time.

But the sentence was—by a disturbing but vivid analogy—trying to convey an important insight about systems theory: Systems are remarkably resilient and persistent. The subsystems that make up the system work together to maintain equilibrium. It is only when multiple subsystems are simultaneously weakened that a system can be brought down.

It's clear to me why that forgotten sentence came back as I was reading Dr. Baker's book. Multiple subsystems in our moral, spiritual, social and civic architecture have been under attack for a long time—if not by explosives, by corrosives.

Companies insert a little corrosion here and there to sell their products: Fear and resentment to sell guns, greed and pride to sell high-status gas-guzzlers, lust to sell pornography, and gluttony to sell high-fat, high-sugar foods.

Political parties drive in little—and sometimes not so little—wedges here and there to win the next election.

Websites, TV networks, and authors weaken trust and spread outrage trying to increase viewers, page-views, and readership.

Ongoing corrosive interventions like these at multiple key junctures could easily produce unintended consequences that could be sudden, unexpected, and disastrous.

And that's why Dr. Baker's ongoing Our Values project—and this new book *United America*—are so important. If we know that some forces threaten our moral, spiritual, social, and civic architecture, we are made responsible by our knowledge to respond. But if we respond merely by attacking those who are part of the problem—often with more ignorance than malice—we will ourselves become part of the problem by infusing more resentment, antagonism, fear, and hostility into the system.

What we need, in words from the Bible's last and most apocalyptic book, is to "wake up and strengthen the things that remain." We need a healing outpouring of positivity, like a healing balm, to neutralize and overcome the corrosive acids of negativity that weaken our moral, spiritual, social and civic architecture.

The question, of course, is: What would such a healing outpouring of positivity look like?

And that's what Dr. Baker tells us in this book.

If we want to strengthen the key subsystems that make up the American system, we will promote the deep values that Americans share. That means that even in disagreement, we will practice civility and a respect for others. We will build on our common ground of both symbolic and critical patriotism. We will emphasize our shared love for freedom, security and self-reliance. We will celebrate equal opportunity, the dream of advancement, and the pursuit of happiness. And we will unite around a sense of wider connectedness.

Just as destructive interventions target multiple points in a system, healing interventions must arise system-wide. That's why Dr. Baker and his colleagues have presented their research in an accessible format that can be used to stimulate conversation all through the system: in churches, in faculty lounges, in libraries, in office conference rooms, in retreat centers, in classrooms, in online chats, around tables over meals.

In your hands, then, you hold a resource that can help you become a kind of reverse-terrorist and nonviolent activist— like "salt and light" to use another phrase from the Bible. You don't have to sit idly by while corrosive forces weaken the ties that bind us together: You can help overcome corrosion with cohesion.

When others try to divide, you can respond positively: "Did you know that some researchers have proven that we Americans hold 10 values in common?"

When others speak in ways that intentionally or unintentionally weaken our shared moral, spiritual, social, and civic architecture, you can respond with an outpouring of healing and affirmation: "That may be true, but I've been reading about the 10 deep values that hold us together. If you'd be interested, I can tell you about them ..."

So, this is a book to be read ... but even more, it's a book to be shared and translated into thousands of healing conversations across America.

Our values matter, and you and I can help them survive and thrive.

You are about to discover how.

—*Brian D. McLaren*

Brian McLaren is a best-selling author who has written more than a dozen books about building bridges across the chasms that can separate religious, cultural and political groups. He also is a frequent guest on television, radio and news media programs, talking about the challenge of peacemaking in a turbulent world.

Introduction by David Crumm

How to Use This Truly Unique Book

The book in your hands is unique—and we don't use that word lightly.

First, this book is unique in subject. Dr. Wayne Baker is reporting a surprising truth about Americans: We are united by Ten Core Values. This truth is empowering because it enables us to rise above and see beyond political polarization, Washington gridlock, the imagery of Red/Blue states, and the rhetoric of culture wars and class warfare. In this turbulent era, publishers are producing a steady flow of books on values, but those books ultimately fall into two piles. In one pile, books focus on conflicts over American values, our so-called "culture wars;" in the other pile are personal manifestos calling for unity around the author's own set of core values. In sharp contrast with the culture-war books, Dr. Baker shows how Americans agree on a surprising number of principles; and in contrast with the personal appeals, this book is based on years of nonpartisan, scientifically balanced polling and research.

Second, this book is exceptional in its format, designed for individual reading and flexible use in classes, small groups and other settings where men and women enjoy civil discussion about the urgent issues of our day. Educators and business leaders will find this book very useful, partly because it is so easy to adapt for each setting. You may choose to read it cover to cover or tailor the book to your particular interests and preferences. You can select the chapters and values you are most eager to read about and read them in any order. Within each chapter you will find topics to contemplate and discuss, along with questions that will stimulate reflection and respectful discussion about a value, what it means, and the challenges of applying it. Even within each chapter, this book is flexible. We encourage you to choose your favorite sub-sections.

If you are reading this as a member of a small group or class, you can custom design reading assignments to cover the material most essential to meet your needs. You can choose questions from this book to ask your group; you can develop your own questions; and you can look online for additional study guides at UnitedAmericaBook.com. This nonpartisan book is designed for easy use in America's public square, whether your forum gathers in a school, a corporate conference room, a library, a coffee shop, a living room or a congregation.

What Are Core Values?

Dr. Baker defines a Core American Value as a value that is strongly held by a large majority of Americans, stable over time, and shared across diverse demographic, religious and political lines.

Values, by definition, are emotional. A strongly held value is a guiding principle that engages the passions. The term "core value" is the same—it conjures the emotions, and can mean different things to different people.

"Core" refers to that which is central, innermost, vital or the most essential part of something. The word derives from the Latin "corpus," meaning body. We speak, for example, of the corpus of literature on a subject. Here, a core value represents an area of deep and broad consensus among the American people, not disagreement and division. A core value is **not** a prescription of what Americans **ought** to believe, but what

Americans *actually* do believe. A core value, as Dr. Baker defines it, has four proven characteristics:

1. It has to be strongly held. People can't be lukewarm on, say, patriotism for it to qualify as a Core American Value.
2. It must be widely held. This means that a large majority of Americans strongly hold a value.
3. The value has to be stable over time. We get the same results across surveys taken at different times.
4. The value doesn't vary much when we compare people of different ages, levels of education, religious affiliations, political differences and so forth. Consider, for example, the type of patriotism called "critical patriotism" (covered in Chapter 10). On a scale of 1 to 5, with 5 being "strongly agree," the average is 4.14 for liberals and 4.25 for conservatives.

The meaning of "core values" can be seized, manipulated and wielded by either side of the political aisle. This book is an attempt to reclaim the concept of "core values" from those who would usurp it, and make it a more neutral term. The idea that we share certain basic values is valuable and empowering—it's an insight that can bridge political chasms rather than deepen them.

How Is the Book Organized?

Each chapter focuses on one of the Ten Core American Values identified by Dr. Baker through four national research surveys.

The first chapter starts with issues of respect for others and civility, because millions of Americans are indicating in polls and in online comments that they are deeply concerned about our apparent lack of respect today. As you read about each Core American Value, you have the opportunity to not only reflect on your own values but also find what you share in common with most Americans. What you will discover is that the vast majority of Americans embrace a significant, distinct set of values. We are not as divided as it appears.

The book closes with a chapter on critical or "tough love" patriotism. It means that when we criticize America and its policies, we do so because we love our nation, want to improve it, and have it live up to American ideals.

After examining the Ten Core American Values, the reader will find much to celebrate about being an American. In addition, the book will challenge Americans to live up to their values and to put into practice what they hold most dear.

What Will I Find in Each Chapter?

The content varies from chapter to chapter, but you always will find: an overview explaining why each value is a "Core American Value" and a story about a personal experience that offers insight into the value and questions for discussion. Many chapters also contain historical information about the particular core value. Keeping these discussions relevant, most chapters include current social issues that are putting a specific value to the test.

Sprinkled throughout each chapter are quotes from famous people, along with comments from OurValues.org readers, who have been discussing these values online. These comments are included to show a range of common opinions you might encounter. They are meant to spark your thoughts and further discussion: Do you resonate with these viewpoints—or disagree with them? Do you have a similar story, experience, or comment?

How Do I Use The Questions?

At the end of each topic are suggested questions for group discussion. You don't have to answer every question. Choose questions most useful for your situation or group. If you are not part of a group, you may choose to keep a personal journal to reflect on the questions.

How you use the questions is up to you. Sometimes when posing a question to a group, it is helpful to first set aside one minute of silence for everyone to think about and compose a response. Some groups expect to "go around the circle" to answer. This can put folks on the spot. You may want to allow participants the option of "when" or "if" they will answer. Aim for balanced participation. You could limit the time each individual has to answer—a three-minute timer works well as a "monitor." Do ask everyone to honor the person speaking by engaging in active listening—listening with the intent to understand, not judge. Ask questions of clarification. As a discussion leader, ask the group to reflect carefully on what they are hearing by quickly paraphrasing what a speaker has just said. This builds the discussion and shows the value of each person's contribution.

Who is Dr. Wayne E. Baker?

Dr. Wayne E. Baker is an American author and sociologist on the senior faculty of the University of Michigan Ross School of Business where he is Chair of the Management & Organizations area and the Robert P. Thome Professor of Business Administration. He is also Professor of Sociology at the University of Michigan and Faculty Associate at the Institute for Social Research.

Dr. Baker is best known both for his research in economic sociology and his research on values, where he documented Americans' core values. His data show that Americans share more core values than news media and political campaigns will admit.

Dr. Baker leads the Americans' Evolving Values project at the University of Michigan Institute for Social Research. The purpose of this project is to create a barometer of American values. This initiative has conducted several national surveys of the values of Americans. The material for this book is based on Dr. Baker's research and survey results.

His earlier book on values, *America's Crisis of Values: Reality and Perception*, earned high praise in reviews by *The New York Times, Christian Century, Political Science Quarterly, American Journal of Sociology*, and other prestigious publications.

Dr. Baker's daily online magazine OurValues.org promotes civil conversation on American ethics and values. Dr. Baker founded OurValues.org in May 2008. He and his occasional contributing writers have published more than 1,500 columns addressing the day's most pressing issues. Some material in this book is reproduced, excerpted, or paraphrased from his blog. Dr. Baker writes in both academic and popular media on this theme of American values and is often invited to present his findings across the United States, and in the media including NPR and C-Span. Dr. Baker is frequently a guest panelist at conferences and university forums.

Dr. Baker earned a Ph.D. in sociology at Northwestern University and was a post-doctoral fellow at Harvard University. Prior to joining the University of Michigan faculty, he was on the faculty of the University of Chicago. He lives in Ann Arbor, Michigan, with his wife, their son, and two Birman cats.

What Are the Sources of the Data Used in This Book?

This book is designed to quickly engage a wide range of readers with fascinating and often provocative insights. The writing style is compelling, often personal, and cuts right to the major findings you'll want to discuss. That means we have removed the complex scientific analysis of these data that would appear in a book designed for an academic audience. However, to be clear, these findings are based on research using the highest standards, followed by exhaustive analyses of these data. Here is a short overview of the book's sources:

The backbone of the book is data collected via four nationally representative surveys of American Values, conducted in 2009 and 2010 by Dr. Baker. These surveys asked about more than two dozen possible core American values. Statistical analyses revealed ten that met the four criteria for a core value. Each chapter in this book presents one of the ten. These surveys were administered by the Survey Research Center at the University of Michigan Institute for Social Research (ISR). They were funded in part by the Carnegie Corporation of New York and ISR.

The results from these four national surveys are supplemented with findings from other surveys that Dr. Baker has conducted, such as the Detroit Arab American Study and Detroit Area Study, as well as surveys by Gallup, Pew Research Center, Public Religion Research Institute, World Values Surveys and others. The chapters also draw on published research in the social sciences. Brief citations are included in the text, with full citations provided at the web site for this book, UnitedAmericaBook.com.

Ultimately, Build a Stronger Community

America is spinning through turbulent changes in our rapidly transforming world. At the same time, our traditional sources of reliably balanced information—including our major newspapers, magazines and bookstores—are collapsing and, in some cases, reappearing in entirely new forms with new missions. We are losing our pillars of neutral media. This is a time when angry voices can sway our impressions of our communities and our nation as a whole. We can fear that America itself is crumbling into warring camps.

In fact, America rests on common ground.

These Ten Core Values form a national foundation for civil dialogue and healthy, cooperative relationships. This book is a unique, transparent window into those guiding principles, but it also is a call to action. Tell friends, neighbors and co-workers. Organize a discussion. Reclaim the truth of our common ground. Build a stronger community.

—*David Crumm*

As a journalist for 40 years, David Crumm has reported on values and religious-and-cultural diversity in the U.S. and around

the world. In 2007, he co-founded ReadTheSpirit online maga-
zine and publishing house, which continues to report on these
vital issues in daily online stories as well as books like United
America.

CHAPTER 1

Respect for Others

"R-E-S-P-E-C-T!" "FIND OUT what it means to me!" These lyrics by Otis Redding were made famous by the Queen of Soul, Aretha Franklin. They make you want to sing and dance. But the idea of respect goes far beyond the lyrics of a popular song: respect for others is one of the Ten Core American values. It is so important that it actually characterizes what it means to be American.

This chapter will take a close look at respect for others: how we define and demonstrate respect (and disrespect!), how ideas about respect for others have changed over time, and how some social issues put this core value to the test.

Defining Respect for Others

What does respect for others mean to you?

A wry definition of respect in the online Urban Dictionary is "a quality seriously lacking in today's society." It's true that we don't always show respect for others, but it is a strong and widely shared principle. It is a value we aspire to live by. Respect for others means esteem and appreciation for all people, regardless of differences in faith, race, ethnicity, sexual orientation or other considerations. Respect is more than tolerance. I may tolerate my neighbor's midnight garage band, but enduring something is different from looking for what's good, right and positive (and then, in this example, negotiating a better music schedule).

This definition of respect implies that there's something worthwhile in the other person, even if we do not agree with the person. It means that we value other points of view. It opens us up to the humanity in others. Americans today disagree on many things, but we are united in the idea that everyone deserves respect—even when we don't personally subscribe to the person's beliefs.

More than 90 percent of Americans in the national surveys I conducted said that respect for people of different racial and ethnic groups is important to them. The same was true when I asked about respect for people of different faiths and religions. Like other core values, the principle of respect for others is shared by young and old, liberals and conservatives, and people of all faiths and religious affiliations.

"I tend to think respect for various cultures is derived from the environment in which you live."

Posted by Tony Abrom on OurValues.org, February 9, 2011.

Respect for others is so strong that it shapes the way we view social issues. For example, attitudes about race and gender issues have become less and less polarized over time, because most Americans today are approaching these issues with a general respect for those who are different from themselves. Approval of black-white marriages has steadily increased since Gallup started asking about this issue in 1958. As of 2011, almost nine of ten Americans (86 percent) approved of these marriages, up from 4 percent in 1958. Same-sex marriage is a divisive issue, but support has increased over time. Today, Gallup polls show that a majority of Americans support legalizing same-sex marriage. Many people have changed their minds about it, switching from oppose to approve. The main reasons, according to a 2013 Pew Research Center survey, are knowing someone who is homosexual or growing more open and tolerant over time. Only 8 percent cite equal rights as the reason. In other words, it's respect for others that has shifted attitudes about same-sex marriage.

Almost all Americans support the principles of religious tolerance and religious freedom. For example, 88 percent of Americans in a 2011 Public Religion Research Institute (PRRI) survey completely or mostly agree that "America was founded on the idea of religious freedom for everyone, including religious groups that are unpopular." The same PRRI survey found that 95 percent of Americans completely or mostly agree with the statement: "All religious books should be treated with respect even if we don't share the religious beliefs of those who use them."

Why is respect for others such an essential principle? The answer might appear to be self-evident, but it's important to be explicit about why it's important that Americans value respect for others. America is a large, diverse, multicultural society. We are a mix of peoples, religions, races, and ethnicities. Elsewhere diversity spells disaster—hostility, hatred, conflict and violence. Here, a strong principle of respect for others mutes these tendencies, encourages respectful treatment of others, and provides a foundation for laws that promote justice and fairness.

> *"Without feelings of respect, what is there to distinguish men from beasts?"*
>
> **Confucius**

Respect for others shapes our identity as Americans. But our specific applications of the principle of respect have changed over time—the next section will take a closer look at this. But the great news is that, in an increasingly diverse and contentious country, the overwhelming majority of us agree that respect for others is indeed a core American value.

- Where in our society have you experienced or witnessed a lack of respect for others?

- Why is respect for others important to you?

- I cited some trends that indicate a growth in respect for others. What would you add to the list?

- Did you ever encounter a situation where it was challenging for you to show respect? How were you changed by this experience?

Who Deserves Respect?

Americans agree with the principle of respect for all people regardless of race, ethnicity, religion, sexual orientation and so on. But, something is changing in the American use of the word "respect" and our decisions about who does (or does not) deserve respect and how to show respect.

"Respect your elders" was an admonition most baby-boomers grew up hearing. Other maxims included "children are to be seen and not heard" and "only speak when spoken to." These sayings were directed toward children. In other words, in the company of adults, "being quiet" was a form of respect. If you weren't brought up in the '40s and '50s these concepts will seem very foreign, even strange. Back then, persons in certain positions were automatically given respect: law enforcement, teachers, clergy, government officials, coaches. The list goes on.

Talk to teenagers today and ask who they respect. Most likely they will respond, "Those who earn my respect." How is respect earned? They respect those who are authentic, honest and fair. Respect is given to people who do what they say, who live according to what they believe, who are persons of integrity. A position or title doesn't necessarily garner respect, but integrity does.

It is easy to understand this shift if we look back over events in the past sixty years. Sixty years ago, the Civil Rights Movement revealed deep-seated racism in all levels of our culture. The Vietnam War and protests against it built a mistrust of government and those in power. Kent State demonstrated that those whose job it was to protect might kill you. Watergate exposed corruption at the highest level—the presidency of the United States. Well-known "televangelists" were exposed for indecency and fraud. The abuse of children by revered figures, including clergy, athletic coaches and scouting leaders, laid bare our worst fears. What event or incident would you add to the list? Title and position no longer guarantee respect. Maybe that's a good thing.

Respect in America today is much more than blind acceptance, allegiance or trust. It is deeper than a superficial nod at civility. When you respect another, you value the person as an individual, as a person of worth. Honor, esteem and appreciation are reflections of respect.

- How does an individual earn your respect these days?

- What causes you to lose respect for an individual?

- Are there people you automatically respect, because of their job, position, or title? Why or why not?

Demonstrating Respect

Do you consider yourself a person who respects others, especially those who are different from you? How do you show your respect? How we live out our core values is extremely important. We can talk all we want about how important something like respect is to us, but our actions can betray our principles. If you are reading this book as part of a group, I encourage you to spend some time together pondering and responding to these questions.

"I like to listen. I have learned a great deal from listening carefully. Most people never listen."

Ernest Hemingway

One way I try to show respect is by attempting to withhold judgment and keeping an open mind. The primary way I do this is by listening. By asking sincere questions and listening with the intent to understand, I begin to know how another person sees the world differently from how I see it, which eventually leads me to a certain level of respect (even though I may not agree!). Questions that put someone on the defensive are not helpful. Most of us know instinctively when we are making genuine inquiries and when our intent is just to prove that we are right and someone else is wrong. Questions to truly gain a better understanding or find common ground often lead to new insight and acceptance of differences. Conversations like this are about creating relationships, not making a particular point. Each person has different practices they use to express respect, although we may not always name them. When we act on our core values, like respect, we create the America we are proud of and want to be identified with.

> *"I am less inclined to protest, 'Why don't you see it the way I do?' and more inclined to say, 'You see it that way? Holy cow! How amazing!'"*
>
> **Robert Fulghum,** *It Was On Fire When I Lay Down On It*

- What are some ways you show respect?

- Was there a time when others showed you respect, even though they disagreed with you or what you were doing?

- When have you felt mutual respect between you and another person whose beliefs are different from yours?

> *"When you practice gratefulness, there is a sense of respect toward others."*
>
> **Dalai Lama**

Core Values Reflected in Character Strengths: Respect and Kindness

Character strengths are good indicators of core values. What are character strengths? Just as physical strength is the capacity in our bodies to exert force, character strengths are the enduring, positive qualities of our intellectual and emotional makeup. Character strengths are things we're noticeably "good at" and that impel us to act in certain ways, such as perseverance, creativity, kindness, fairness, humility and hope. The VIA Institute on Character lists twenty-four different character strengths.

Individuals, groups of people, and even entire nations develop and hold character strengths. America is no exception. As a nation and culture, we share a sense of "national character"—the enduring qualities of heart and mind that are the American people. Defining and strengthening our national character has been a central focus in American life since the founding of our nation.

A global survey of character strengths helps us identify and discuss America's character strengths. Psychologists Nansook Park, Chris Peterson and Martin Seligman developed a survey of twenty-four character strengths that represent six universal virtues: wisdom and knowledge, courage, humanity, justice, temperance and transcendence. More than 100,000 people from fifty-four nations took the survey, including Americans in all fifty states.

What do you think is America's No. 1 character strength? These researchers discovered that *kindness* is the top character strength. It's one of the character strengths associated with the virtue of humanity: kindness is an interpersonal strength that involves helping, taking care of and befriending others.

"Kindness is the language which the deaf can hear and the blind can see."

Mark Twain

Are you surprised to learn that kindness tops America's list? What surprised me was that kindness was not the top strength anywhere else in the world. Among the fifty-four nations included in the survey, it was only in America that kindness earned the top spot. Kindness logically flows out of respect for others. Showing kindness to others is the action behind the core value of respect.

"Constant kindness can accomplish much. As the sun makes ice melt, kindness causes misunderstanding, mistrust and hostility to evaporate."

Albert Schweitzer

- Describe a time when someone unexpectedly showed kindness toward you.

- Why do you think that kindness is America's top character strength? Did this surprise you?

- When have you felt that Americans were not kind or respectful?

- In a typical day, how kind and respectful are the people you encounter?

Respect and America's Moral Character

Kindness is embraced as our top character strength. We overwhelmingly agree that kindness is a good thing. Despite our agreement on the importance of kindness, not all of us are convinced that the rest of America is well-intentioned. Americans seem to have a cynical view of the state of moral values in our country. The goal of strengthening American character is a recurring and major theme on any campaign trail: politicians cite the decline of American character and values as the culprits behind many social and economic problems. But how true is this?

The most striking finding in a 2012 Gallup survey was that only 20 percent of Americans said moral values were good or excellent. Everyone else said they were poor or only fair.

When Gallup asked people to describe the problem in their own words, first on the list was "Lack of tolerance, compassion, consideration of others, respect, and caring." I find this fascinating because respect for others and concerns about the welfare of others are among the top Core American Values, according to my national surveys. If "kindness" is the number one character strength of Americans, how can "lack of … compassion … and caring" be a major problem? Putting Gallup's findings and mine together indicates a wide gap between our values and the reality we encounter in our day-to-day lives.

"Preservation of one's own culture does not require contempt or disrespect for other cultures."

Cesar Chavez

Most Americans say the state of our moral values is deplorable and tumbling downhill. Incivility is the number one reason Americans give for their dark assessment of American morals. We share principles like respect for others, but we often differ in opinions about how these values should be applied. What, for example, does respect for others mean in healthcare reform or immigration reform? We choose "kindness" as the top character strength to define "American" but at the same time point to our lack of compassion and care as a problem. Clearly we are a nation struggling with our differences.

"But every difference of opinion is not a difference of principle."

Thomas Jefferson

- How would you rate the state of moral values in America today?

- How do you define America's character strengths?

- How would you rate your own moral character?

- Why do we prize kindness and respect for others, but also see lack of compassion and care as widespread problems?

Respect and the 'New Civility'

We just read that "Lack of tolerance, compassion, consideration of others, respect, and caring" were cited as the top reasons for moral decline in America. People feel like there is a general climate of incivility in our culture. In response, many groups are organizing events to promote respect and consideration between those of different ethnic, religious and political groups.

I participated as a panelist in a civility experiment in Chicago in 2011. "The (Un)Common Good" was a series of new programs sponsored by the Illinois Humanities Council.

"We desperately need to continue a discussion of civility in this country."

Posted by Cindy L. on OurValues.org, January 30, 2011.

Here's how the Council describes the program's mission: "We're presenting The (Un)Common Good series because we believe there is an urgent need to re-imagine new ways to discuss issues across ideologies, to model civil debate and dialogue between people who come down on different sides of an issue, and to share information that strives to be unbiased, fact-based and even-handed. We think that engagement with the humanities is a vehicle through which we can talk, listen and disagree."

Part of the role of the panel was to challenge assumptions about the ideological segregation and polarized discussion in America today. My challenge was to address this: Are we really as polarized as we think? Are Americans really deeply divided when it comes to our most important values? There's no doubt that politicians, party activists, and political elites are deeply divided and getting more so. But what about the rest of us? What about what social scientists unflatteringly call the "masses"?

Forgive me if I seem to be a bit of a populist, but I think what average Americans believe is as important as what our politicians believe. When we look at what the "masses" believe, we find wide areas of agreement when it comes to the most important values. Moreover, many beliefs are converging over time, such as beliefs about race and gender issues. Why do we still perceive a culture of incivility? Sociologist Paul DiMaggio thinks Americans may have developed "chronic habits of mind that render us ill equipped to assess the strength of the social fabric." We too easily assume that public conflicts, incivility in politics and the ill-tempered rhetoric of our political leaders mean that most Americans are just as hostile and divided. Put aside the fury of our leaders and you can start to see the core values underlying American society.

- How do you remain civil in your relationships and dialogue?

- Are you part of any organized efforts in civility?

- Is the general public as polarized as politicians? Why or why not?

- How did recent political campaigns affect your personal relationships with those of opposing political parties?

Is Respect for Others Just Lip Service?

Although an overwhelming majority of Americans say that respect for different races, ethnicities, and religions are important to them, a new body of research offers intriguing insights. Here's the key question: Is respect for minorities just lip service? Is this respect really a core value—or just empty words that mask true feelings of prejudice or even hatred?

Academics never use a short word when a long one is available. Lip service, in survey-research lingo, is called "social desirability." It's the tendency for people to say what they think they should say—what's desirable or proper rather than what they really feel. As Caitlin, one reader of my blog, commented on Feb. 9, 2011, "I have a hard time believing that respect for all people, regardless of their background, is something that most Americans TRULY value. Of course most Americans are going to agree to this as a value when it's a matter of checking a box on a survey, but when it comes to putting it into practice in our real lives, there's no way we constantly choose the path of respect. The most privileged members of society consistently marginalize the most oppressed—that doesn't sound like respect to me."

Respect for others could just be lip service, but new research by my colleagues at the University of Michigan provides some insights. They published results from a series of studies about multiculturalism and diversity, issues that tend to put respect for others to the test. They found that white Americans are likely to resist workplace initiatives around these issues.

Does this indicate underlying prejudice? Does this expose a lack of respect? Here's what the lead researcher, Jeffrey Sanchez-Burks, concludes: "Our research reveals that this resistance can have little to do with prejudice. Instead, it can stem from a basic human need to belong." Diversity initiatives are supposed to be about inclusion, but when these are framed in the language of multiculturalism, whites feel excluded. That's why they resist. Indeed, the stronger a person's need to belong, the more they resist initiatives that appear to exclude them.

"I've been thinking lately that it's not so much about a positive view of "wanting to belong" but much more about a negative fear of "being excluded."

Posted by John Hawthorne on OurValues.org, Feb 10, 2011.

What if diversity initiatives are framed as colorblindness? Multiculturalism emphasizes differences; colorblindness emphasizes sameness—that categories don't matter and should be ignored. Framed this way, the researchers say that whites feel more included and hence more likely to support such initiatives.

Perhaps when the focus becomes more about what we share in common (like the need to belong) and less about differences, people are able to be more respectful of others. If we value respect for others, we will pursue understanding and acceptance.

- What have been your experiences of "wanting to belong" or "being excluded"?

- Have you ever been in a situation where you felt you were in the minority? (This may include gender, race, political views or religious beliefs.)

- If you have been in the minority, what were your feelings? Did you feel treated differently from the majority? How?

- If you are typically in the majority, in what ways have you been aware of minorities who are present and what they may be experiencing?

Can We Change a Culture of Incivility?

Many Americans are voicing concern over rising incivility in our lives. Where does incivility come from—and how might it be changed?

Following the tragic shootings in Tucson on Jan. 8, 2011, there was talk of a new civility in politics after years of increasingly polarized rhetoric. This tragedy shook some of our leaders into the recognition of the destructiveness of incivility. Sen. Gabrielle Giffords was critically injured from a gunshot wound to her head, reported to be an assassination attempt. Thirteen people were injured and six others killed. A controversial aspect of the incident was the inclusion of Giffords on Sarah Palin's "target list" of those to be unseated from office.

Former Alaska governor Palin made public a map showing twenty House Democrats to be unseated, using a "crosshairs" image to identify them. Many accused Palin of inciting violence through the use of the crosshairs image; her response on Twitter was "Don't retreat, instead—RELOAD!" The political world is one place in our culture where incivility has a history of running wild.

Yet even in politics, there is hope of a culture change. One nod toward civility was Republicans and Democrats sitting side by side during the 2011 State of the Union address following the Tucson incident. It was just a step. There is a strain of incivility in our culture that will have to be transformed before a new civility can dawn.

What might change the shared beliefs, values and behaviors that make up the culture of incivility? Changing any culture is exceedingly difficult. There are enormous forces allied with the status quo. But cultures can change.

Mark DeMoss, self-described as a "conservative evangelical Southern Baptist," and Lanny Davis, a liberal, launched an effort to get members of Congress to sign a "civility pledge." In early 2009, the duo formed the CivilityProject.org. The "Civility Pledge" was a 32-word document sent to all sitting members of Congress.

Here's the pledge:

- I will be civil in my public discourse and behavior.
- I will be respectful of others whether or not I agree with them.
- I will stand against incivility when I see it.

How many members of Congress do you suppose signed it? 100? 200? Maybe more? Actually, only three did: Sen. Joe Lieberman, an independent, and Reps. Frank Wolfe and Sue Myrick, both Republicans.

Due to the lack of interest, DeMoss and company decided to shut down the Civility Project. DeMoss says he hasn't given up on civility, but a title on his blog is "Don't Expect Civility!"

Here is another example of incivility from the political arena. Politics have never been pretty, but the uproar over healthcare reform brought public incivility to a new high. Most of us unfortunately saw and heard it in the news: "You lie!" blurted out by South Carolina Rep. Joe Wilson during President Obama's 2009 address to Congress on healthcare. Wilson claimed it was a spontaneous response when Obama said healthcare reforms would not include insurance coverage for illegal immigrants. Some thought Wilson's comment was planned.

"Kill the bill!" That's what protesters in the congressional visitors' gallery yelled, which wouldn't have been so bad except that some Republican members of Congress cheered them on.

Then, before the historic vote, Tea Party protestors yelled the N-word at African American members of Congress, and anti-homosexual slurs at gay congressional Democrats.

"Baby killer!" That's what Republican Randy Neugenhauer said to Bart Stupak, the pro-life Michigan Democrat who switched his vote in favor of the bill in return for assurances about abortion language. Neugenhauer claimed he said, "It's a baby killer," referring to the bill, not Stupak, but Stupak disagreed. "I've been forwarded a number of emails with language that rivals these public episodes, including the charge of 'treason' for Obama," reported Stupak. This episode of incivility was picked up and repeated by many media outlets.

Does incivility serve some purpose? When a situation persists, it must serve a function. What might it be?

We have what appears to be a contradictory situation. Politicians, political elites, and party activists are increasingly polarized, moving farther apart from one another. Yet public opinion polls clearly show that Americans loathe the divisiveness. And, the values of most Americans are not polarized. There is widespread agreement among Americans when it comes to core values. Which means our polarizing politicians are becoming less and less representative of our actual views.

Yet the culture of incivility persists. Why? Could it be that incivility is fun? I don't mean to be facetious. We don't throw out the divisive elements from Congress. So, at some level, we must want them there. Perhaps verbal duels have replaced the lethal pistol duels that used to take place between political adversaries. Does incivility in Washington make for high-quality reality TV?

"Yes, to a certain degree it is "fun." It's entertaining for the masses to watch two diametrically opposed verbal combatants slug it out. It brings in TV viewers and ratings—which are all important for the paying advertisers. However, none of that helps us solve our real problems."

Posted by Vogon_poem_lover on OurValues.org, January 27, 2011.

Incivility is an easy way to make a career in politics. Rather than developing an educated and nuanced view, a candidate only has to take sides and deliver the scripted rhetoric. It's a convenient shortcut to a political career.

- Is incivility fun?

- Aside from well-publicized episodes of incivility, what have you personally seen and heard?

- How do you have a civil conversation on a controversial issue with someone who has a different opinion?

- Is free speech more important than respect?

Love Thy Neighbor?

Respect for others is an American ideal. But it gets complicated when we apply the ideal to hot-button issues such as race and immigration.

Does the value of respect extend to making a path to citizenship for immigrants who came to America illegally? What does the value of respect for others mean for undocumented immigrants who face deportation and will have to leave behind their American-born children? More than six out of ten Americans (63 percent) say that we should make a path to citizenship, according to a 2013 Public Religion Research Institute poll.

Even some American citizens are not accepted as full members of American society. Consider the situation of Arab- and Muslim-Americans. Many are American-born or naturalized citizens. But their right to belong is still contested. For some, "Arab" and "American" are not compatible. The same feeling exists for "Muslim" and "American" or "Latino" and "American."

"We are a country formed by the melting pot of peoples, so should our values reflect that mix."

Posted by Peter Olsen on OurValues.org, July 10, 2008.

Mainstream Americans are less accepting of Arab-Americans than any other minority group, including African-Americans, Hispanics or Asians. They prefer more "social distance" from Arab-Americans than from anyone else. For example, they'd rather have anyone as a neighbor other than an Arab-American. That's a harsh assessment, but it's what Reynolds Farley and colleagues learned in a Detroit area survey conducted a few years after 9/11.

When asked to think of the racial-ethnic mix of their ideal neighborhood, more people excluded Arab-Americans from their ideal neighborhood than any other group. The survey asked people to rate different groups on a "feeling thermometer." Ratings between 50 and 100 degrees indicate warm or favorable feelings; ratings between 0 and 50 degrees indicate cool or unfavorable feelings. Of all the racial and ethnic groups considered, Arab-Americans received the "coolest" ratings.

"The belief in America is that only "brown skin" immigrants are harmful and need be regulated to protect America. Has anyone noticed that no one complains about the "white-skin" immigrant coming to America?"

Posted by unattributed on OurValues.org.

Even Arab-Americans who are legal citizens don't feel fully accepted or afforded the same protections as other citizens. Legal citizenship does not automatically grant acceptance by mainstream culture. Arab-Americans have not yet received full acceptance. For instance, about half of the general population supports increasing surveillance of Arab-Americans, according to a Detroit area study I conducted. About 40 percent support the detention of suspicious Arabs or Muslims even without sufficient evidence to prosecute them.

My Experience

Not long ago, I drove from Ann Arbor to downtown Detroit for a meeting in a large office building. After parking, I carried two boxes of materials into the building. A security guard promptly stopped me, politely (and firmly) requesting to inspect the boxes. When he finished the inspection, he thanked me. I thanked him in return for doing his job. "Well, it's really important since 9/11," he said. "You know who lives right over there." He raised his eyebrows and cocked his head in the direction of Dearborn.

Dearborn borders Detroit, and it's the location of a highly visible Arab-American enclave. The greater Detroit region is home to one of the oldest and largest Arab communities in North America. I was startled by his statement. "What do you mean?" I asked. He leaned close and whispered, "You know what I mean. All those … Arabs … over there in Dearborn. You can't be too careful."

This encounter represents the "social distance" I mentioned above. Can you imagine what the encounter would have been like for someone from Dearborn?

"The U.S. is the nation it is BECAUSE of the diversity present here. After already celebrating this for hundreds of years, let's not turn our backs on this now."

Posted by Gayle on OurValues.org, May 7, 2012.

An Arab-American woman from Detroit wrote about both her pride in America's melting pot and living with her religious and cultural distinctiveness (see next comment). She sees the melting pot as blending cultures, but still celebrating our individual faiths and cultures. Can the American melting pot be both a closely connected community and also allow for, as she exemplifies, a proud Muslim, wearing the hijab, and working in corporate America?

> *"As an American-born and raised Muslim, wearing the hijab head cover, working in corporate America, I am proud to blend into the melting pot of our diverse metropolitan area, and appreciate all efforts to promote awareness of cultural and religious differences through education."*
>
> **Posted by Faten on OurValues.org, 2008.**

Can Arab-Americans, Muslim-Americans and Latino-Americans be embraced and respected by other Americans? These groups remain suspended between "belonging" and "not belonging" in America.

- What's the racial-ethnic mix of your ideal neighborhood?

- Where do you put Arab- and Muslim-Americans on your "feeling thermometer"?

- Where do you put White, Black or Latino-Americans?

- What would you say is the "litmus test" of your respect for others?

Summarizing Respect for Others

Respect for others—people of different races, religions, sexual orientations, and so on—is a fundamental American value. Respect and kindness are distinguishing American character traits. Yet Americans report a wide gap between the value of respect for others and the practice of respect in everyday life. Our political leaders seem to have lost the value of respect for others. Many Americans struggle with incompatible feelings and values when it comes to issues such as immigration and race. Feelings about Arab- and Muslim-Americans are prime examples. The challenge we face is to integrate respect into our daily lives both as individual Americans and as a nation.

Online resources to explore the topic of respect for others are available at UnitedAmericaBook.com and include materials for group activities and online reader discussions.

CHAPTER 2

Symbolic Patriotism

PATRIOTISM—LOVE OF COUNTRY—IS a vital and widely held Core American Value. Patriotism is an emotional attachment to a place, people, and way of life. George Orwell said there is a spiritual need for patriotism, because we have a desire to feel like we are a part of something immortal.

Love of country is especially strong in America. More than 65 percent of Americans say they are very proud to be American, according to the World Values Survey. This is much higher than many European nations. Among the lowest are Germans (only 22 percent say they are very proud to be German), the Dutch (27 percent) and the French (30 percent).

"We identify the flag with almost everything we hold dear on earth, peace, security, liberty, our family, our friends, our home. … But when we look at our flag and behold it emblazoned with all our rights we must remember that it is equally a symbol of our duties. Every glory that we associate with it is the result of duty done."

Calvin Coolidge

Patriotism elicits an array of feelings and opinions. Symbolic patriotism refers to feelings stirred by national symbols. It is an especially potent form of patriotism in America. Symbolic patriotism is one of the Ten Core Values.

In this chapter, we will explore the special meanings American symbols like the flag and national anthem have in our society. I will address what we know from surveys of Americans about these national symbols, why being an American is an ideological commitment, where American symbols came from in the first place and how Americans react to the real or perceived misuses of American symbols.

Defining Symbolic Patriotism

Almost all Americans feel good when they see Old Glory flying or hear *The Star-Spangled Banner*. These symbols and the emotions they evoke represent the psychological dimension of national identity: the powerful emotional bonds that so many Americans feel for our country. When American symbols stir positive emotions in us, we are connected to one another and to the ideals for which the nation stands.

"The red and white and starry blue, Is freedom's shield and hope."

John Philip Sousa

Our emotions about American symbols are complex and our affection for them can change, depending on how the symbols are used, misused or even abused. Seeing the flag or hearing the anthem quickens my pulse. When writing about symbolic patriotism and its role in American life, I didn't think I would have a personal story to share about this core value. But, here it is!

One summer, I did something that some might think is unpatriotic: I removed the large American flag and flagpole from the stern of my family's sailboat. I did this for safety reasons: the pole was in the way of safe movement and lines often fouled on it. My wife and I discussed this before making the decision to remove it.

But here's why I'm telling you about it. At first, this decision seemed simple, even trivial. But my wife and I both were surprised by the mix of strong feelings it raised in us. We looked around and noticed how many boats flew the flag. What will the other sailors think of us if we remove the flag? What kind of a message would we send to our young son? What we found ourselves wrestling with is symbolic patriotism. My wife and I were feeling the powerful associations that revolve around American symbols.

- How do you feel when you see the American flag flying or hear the national anthem?

- What circumstances have changed your reactions to American symbols?

- When and where have you felt very patriotic? Tell about a time when your feelings of patriotism were kindled.

- What American symbols do you revere and find particularly meaningful? Why?

Symbolic Patriotism: What Americans Say

The Star-Spangled Banner and the American flag are powerful symbols. They elicit strong positive emotions in most people. How do we know Americans feel that way? One way is through surveys. In each of four national surveys of American values, I asked about the importance of flag and anthem.

Almost all Americans, often more than 90 percent, agreed that it made them feel good when they saw the American flag flying. Six of ten felt very strongly about it. This high level of agreement was about the same for hearing *The Star-Spangled Banner.*

"*The flag never meant much to me. Then I moved to England. I was rather surprised by my reaction when I first saw an American flag flying in England. It was a very large flag flying at the American cemetery in Cambridge. I got goose-bumps. Each time I saw an American flag flying in England, one of my first thoughts was 'home.' It was a symbol of much I loved and had left behind. I noticed, and was moved by, every US flag I saw during my time in England since I didn't see it every day. I have since moved back to the States and I find, once again, that the flag doesn't mean as much to me anymore. I believe that the overuse of the American flag here makes it easy to overlook. It's everywhere, on everything. It loses some of its meaning in this overuse. The flag meant much to me when I lived abroad, but I get so many people waving the flag in my face here that I find that it means less to me now that I'm back in the States.*"

Posted by Michelle F. on OurValues.org, June 14, 2010.

Positive feelings about flag and anthem actually grew stronger over time. I wasn't too surprised by these results. Here's what was surprising: in the first survey, symbolic patriotism—a combination of feelings about flag and anthem—was the strongest value we measured. Symbolic patriotism was stronger, or more important to Americans, than freedom or achievement or any other value.

But then, six months later, even though feelings about flag and anthem grew stronger—they came in second place in the overall ranking of values. What edged out symbolic patriotism? The high percentage of Americans who said their financial security was very important to them. The poor state of the economy eclipsed the strength of Americans' positive reactions to American symbols.

- Look at the Table of Contents—each chapter title is a Core American Value. Would you put symbolic patriotism as your strongest value? Why or why not?

- How important is patriotism to you personally?

- How do you show patriotism?

The United States of America: An 'Ideological Commitment'

Why are American symbols like Old Glory and *The Star-Spangled Banner* so important? Why does seeing the flag or hearing the national anthem touch the hearts of so many Americans? And why does any disrespect of these symbols infuriate people?

There's a larger, distinctive meaning behind our national symbols that fuels our strong feelings. That meaning is tied to our national identity–the collective sentiment or feeling of belonging to the same people.

"The things that the flag stands for were created by the experiences of a great people. Everything that it stands for was written by their lives. The flag is the embodiment, not of sentiment, but of history."

Woodrow Wilson

National symbols play an important role in every society. People identify with them. They display them with pride. National symbols represent the unity of a people. The Union Jack, for example, is made up of the individual flags of England, Scotland and Northern Ireland.

On a recent trip to Kenya, a colleague of mine was describing this book and the concept of symbolic patriotism to local friends. When she asked them what national symbols evoke feelings of patriotism for them, they were a bit bewildered, although they agreed their national anthem stirs feelings of love of country. As a rather young country, only fifty-plus years from independence, Kenyans still experience tribal loyalties and conflicts. They are working on a more positive national identity.

National symbols play a special role in American society. Most other nations are what we call "birthright nations." In birthright nations, the feeling of belonging to a "people" comes from common ancestry, history, customs, language and religion. America, however, is not a birthright nation. The sense of belonging to the American people comes from a commitment to a set of ideas and ideals. "Being an American is an ideological commitment," as renowned political scientist Seymour Martin Lipset so aptly put it.

Here's a way to appreciate the difference: Could I become French? If I moved to France, learned perfect French, and became a legal French citizen, would the French accept me as one of them? No. Even if my children were born there, they wouldn't be accepted as French. I would have to be born French to be French. Now reverse the situation. Could a Frenchman (or woman) come to the United States and become an American? Absolutely.

Being American isn't about a common ancestry, history, language, or religion. It's about an ideological commitment, or a loyalty to shared values, aspirations, expectations, and actions. That's why American symbols are so important: they represent a common ideological commitment. And in America, that's the main thing that makes us a people.

- What ideals do you identify as basic to being an American?

- What shared ideas or ideals are most important to you?

The American Flag as Symbol

The American flag is the primary symbol of American patriotism. The Stars and Stripes symbolizes our values and our national identity. Americans "rally 'round the flag." The flag resonates not only with the symbols incorporated in the original design (the use of stars, stripes and colors), but also the meaning that has been attached through time and events. The flag has been raised in times of pride and protest, devotion and destruction, celebration and crisis to communicate what it means to be American.

"Sure I wave the American flag. Do you know a better flag to wave? Sure I love my country with all her faults. I'm not ashamed of that, never have been, never will be."

John Wayne

The American flag was originally created to identify ships and forts. In the early years, private citizens (except captains of ships at sea) did not fly the flag or use it to express patriotism or national identity. We may find it hard to imagine, but prior to the War of 1812 other symbols of patriotism were more prominent, as historian David Hackett Fischer describes in his book *Liberty and Freedom*. Consider that the "Liberty Cap" and eagle were recognized as significant symbols of patriotism and national identity in the early years of the Republic. How many of us even know what the "Liberty Cap" is? Once a symbol of a freed slave in ancient times, it appears on many official U.S. seals and numerous engravings from the American Revolution. This symbol of freedom appears on half-cent and one-penny coins from the 1700s. This once powerful symbol lacks meaning for us today.

> *"We take the stars from heaven, the red from our mother country, separating it by white stripes, thus showing that we have separated from her, and the white stripes shall go down to posterity, representing our liberty."*
>
> **George Washington**

National symbols evolve over time and take on new meaning based on experience, function and history. Objects assume particular significance, and the result is personal feelings that we attach to the object. Each of us endows national symbols with personal meaning.

> *"I'm a retired U.S. Air Force Officer, and the Flag is a great symbol of the United States that I supported throughout my Air Force career. Why else would I put my life on the line if it weren't for something greater than myself? The Flag is that symbol of country and our 'American Way of Life.'"*
>
> **Posted by D. Crouch on OurValues.org, June 14, 2010.**

Gen. George Marshall, American military commander during WWII, made this statement about the American flag: "We are determined that before the sun sets on this terrible struggle, our flag will be recognized throughout the world as a symbol of freedom on the one hand and of overwhelming force on the other."

Do you recall the vivid image after 9/11 of firefighters, covered in ash and soot, raising "Old Glory" amidst the destruction? Another evocative image was the Reuters building in Times Square, also showing the American flag in an expression of solidarity, but then making the decision to remove it, fearing that its display might endanger Reuter journalists around the globe.

More than 80 percent of Americans displayed the flag after 9/11, according to various surveys. The flag flew everywhere: office buildings, factories, homes, cars and clothing. The surge in flag displays could have been a sign of patriotism or a sign of nationalism, the uncritical "blind love" type of patriotism. But psychologist Linda Skitka revealed that the overwhelming motivation was patriotism—love of country and solidarity with fellow Americans.

One of the most recognizable, iconic photographs of the flag is the "Raising the Flag on Iwo Jima" from 1945. Joe Rosenthal won a Pulitzer Prize for Photography for this wartime photo of five U.S. Marines and a U.S. Navy corpsman atop Mount Suribachi in World War II. The U.S. Marine Corps named Rosenthal an honorary Marine, and, after his death, awarded him the Distinguished Public Service Medal.

Another memorable American flag photo was taken on July 20, 1969 … on the moon. Apollo 11 astronauts Neil Armstrong and Buzz Aldrin, the first humans on the moon, planted the American flag. The iconic image shows Aldrin saluting the flag. Subsequent Apollo missions also planted flags, and some of them are still standing today.

American flags popped up all over Joplin, Missouri, when the town was ravaged by one of the deadliest tornadoes in American history. It was a public display of hope and resilience. One Joplin resident planted an American flag on the rubble pile that had once been his business. He told the media: "We're Americans, and we can make it through anything. We're still standing."

The American flag can be a beacon for those seeking political asylum, refuge from war, or better economic prospects. But, it can also be used as a giant KEEP OUT sign. For example, activists place American flags along the U.S.-Mexico border wall to symbolize their opposition to illegal immigration. Time Magazine pictured the border wall on a 2008 cover, calling it "The Great Wall of America." Like the Chinese version, it is meant to keep people out—and American symbols are used to reinforce the idea.

"It is the flag just as much of the man who was naturalized yesterday as of the men whose people have been here many generations."

Henry Cabot Lodge

The American flag, universally recognized as a symbol of liberty and freedom, has also been used as a weapon of hatred and racism. Stanley Forman, a photojournalist for Boston's Herald American, captured the moment on April 5, 1976, when a crowd of white teenagers rushed Ted Landsmark, a young black lawyer, and one of them tried to impale Landsmark with the staff point of an American flag. The circumstances of this event are described in the book *The Soiling of Old Glory: The Story of a Photograph That Shocked America.* The photo is on the book's cover.

Images of the flag evoke a variety of feelings. Each of us brings our own experiences and memories that flavor our reactions to the Stars and Stripes waving in the breeze. You may associate universal qualities of freedom, democracy, or sacrifice at seeing the flag, or it might arouse a very personal sentiment of security or gratitude. And for some, it may conjure negative feelings from the times the nation did not live up to its ideals. Not all Americans revere the flag.

- Close your eyes and picture the flag. What first came to mind? Describe the image.

- When have you felt proud at seeing the 'Stars and Stripes' fly?

- What does the flag mean to you?

Old Glory and Flag Day

Throughout many eras, the flag has been a powerful American symbol. Across the board, seeing Old Glory warms Americans' hearts. It is such a significant American symbol that the U.S. Congress set aside June 14, the day the flag was adopted in 1777, to commemorate the occasion. Flag Day is not an official federal holiday (so you don't get the day off from work) but it is an official observance. I admit that Flag Day is not an observance I routinely remember. I know when it is Flag Day only because U.S. holidays and observances appear automatically in my Google calendar.

Flag Day is a bigger deal in some places than others. Some communities give small American flags to their schoolchildren to carry throughout the day. According to various sources, the oldest Flag Day parade takes place in the small town of Fairfield, Washington, and the largest in Troy, New York.

"The Flag is very important to me. I recognize Flag Day every June 14th, but I also recognize the Flag every day. I wear a miniature flag in my lapel almost every time I wear a suit, and I salute the flag and treat it with proper respect on all occasions."

Posted by D. Crouch on OurValues.org, June 14, 2010.

In researching Flag Day, I learned even more about the symbol we call Old Glory. That nickname for the flag turns up in various eras of American history, including a post-9/11 photo exhibition. The famous nickname, Old Glory, originated with a 19th-century sea captain, William Driver, from Salem, Massachusetts. According to most accounts, the flag was a gift from his mother and some young women in Salem. He flew it first from his whaling ship, the *Charles Doggett*. When he raised it, Driver said, "I name thee Old Glory."

Years later, Driver retired in Nashville, Tennessee, where his flag became a popular American landmark. He often displayed it on patriotic occasions. When the Civil War broke out, the South controlled Tennessee. Driver feared that Confederate soldiers and secessionists would try to find and destroy Old Glory. He hid the 30' by 42' flag by sewing it into his bed cover. By the time the war was over, the flag had become a nationally famous symbol.

Driver's Old Glory was inherited by his family. In 1922, the family donated it to the Smithsonian Institution. In 1999, conservators at the Smithsonian began a three-year, $18 million project to restore the flag, as reported in *Science News*. The restoration can only be described as loving and reverential.

The noteworthy question in this story: why did this particular flag become significant? How did it become a popular American symbol? In this case, it gained value through a sequence of historic events. The meaning of the flag evolved over time.

- Do you and your family observe Flag Day?

- What does your community do to celebrate Flag Day?

- Tell a story or experience when a particular flag took on new meaning or significance for you.

Reactions to Real or Perceived Misuse of the Flag

Almost all Americans say that seeing Old Glory makes them feel good. The reverse is also true: many are angered by the misuse of the flag. But sometimes misuse is a matter of perception and perspective.

The flag took on new meanings in the American Civil War. The north "searched for emblems of its sacred cause," says Fischer, "and found them in old American symbols." The American flag was the chief one. Northerners rallied around Old Glory, seeing it as a symbol of national unity and freedom for all. Southerners were infuriated by this new-found significance, says Fischer, and went out of their way to defile it. This included a party in Murfreesboro, Tennessee, where the dance floor was covered with American flags and danced upon. Other places in the South organized ritual flag burnings.

"Did a man ever fight for a holier cause, Than Freedom and Flag, and Equal Laws?"

Northern Rallying Cry, quoted by Fischer in Liberty and Freedom.

If you see a tattered American flag, how does it make you feel? Look around, especially after the Fourth of July or Memorial Day when more flags are flying. You'll see plenty of faded, ripped and torn American flags still flying. Does it make you feel ashamed or angry—or indifferent?

Seeing a torn flag upsets many people, like a 30-year member of the Fraternal Order of Eagles when he returned home to Michigan after wintering in Arizona. He was appalled to find a ripped American flag still flying over the chapter's lodge. He took it upon himself to replace it at his own expense. He claims he was suspended because of the situation, though the group disputes his claim. Claims aside, what do you think of his action? Should he be congratulated for taking the initiative to replace the torn flag?

The United States Flag Code spells out in great detail how the flag should be handled and cared for. There are many standards of respect. The flag should not be displayed as decoration, used to cover a ceiling, for advertising, as an article of clothing, stepped on and so forth. Proper display requires that it be flown only from sunrise to sunset, though if doing so would heighten patriotic effect, it can be displayed at night—provided it is properly illuminated. The flag should never be allowed to touch the ground. It is to be raised briskly and lowered ceremoniously.

A flag that is no longer serviceable should be disposed of properly. If you see a tattered or dirty flag, you can report it online to Flag Keepers, a voluntary organization, and they will contact the owner or occupant of the building.

The Flag Code is law, but it is rarely enforced. The flag is often used in advertising, on clothes, picnic ware, and so forth. Pop celebrities Kesha, Rihanna and Kendall Jenner are some of the latest to wear flag shorts. There are flag pants, T-shirts, robes, dresses, shorts, bikinis, underwear and baby clothes. Some people consider them disrespectful; others think they're stylish.

All are violations of the code. But the U.S. Supreme Court considers enforcing the code to be a violation of free speech. So, we are pretty much free to do whatever we want with the flag. In spite of this freedom, most Americans find misuse of the flag very upsetting.

"We do not consecrate the flag by punishing its desecration, for in doing so we dilute the freedom this cherished emblem represents."

William J. Brennan

Sometimes use or misuse is in the eyes of the beholder. Of all the things that can trip up a presidential candidate during the long run to the White House, patriotism usually is not one of them. But it happened to Barack Obama in the 2008 presidential campaign. The questions revolved around American symbols. Rumors spread about Obama removing an American flag lapel pin and replacing an image of the American flag on his campaign jet with the campaign logo. Other rumors claimed that Obama wouldn't say the Pledge of Allegiance or place his hand over his heart when he did. Some said he "saluted" the flag with an intentional "crotch salute": hands clasped, held below the waist.

Some rumors proved to be true. He did remove the flag lapel pin—and more than once. The first time was to signal his opposition to the Iraq war. It's also true that he replaced the image of the American flag on his campaign jet, but Urban Legends notes that the image was part of the corporate logo of North American Airlines (the owner of the jet). A new version of this rumor circulated in 2012. It claimed that after Obama became president, he replaced the American flag on Air Force One with his logo. Not true, says Urban Legends.

Most rumors were not true, but Obama felt compelled to defend his patriotism throughout the campaign. He gave speeches about patriotism, such as one delivered in Harry Truman's hometown of Independence, Missouri. The Obama Campaign created a web site, "Fight the Smears," to dispel rumors. One video clip showed Obama leading the Pledge of Allegiance in the U.S. Senate with his hand over his heart. Urban Legends investigated the "crotch salute" and declared it a hoax, but many critics remained unconvinced.

Flag displays can be questioned for their sincerity, purpose, or meaning. For some, the flag represents the failure of America to live up to its ideals: unjust or unnecessary wars, racism and poverty at home, an unjustified sense of moral superiority. Some universities banned displays of the flag after 9/11, fearing that it might be offensive or insensitive to a culturally and nationally diverse population of students, staff and faculty. And, some Americans questioned the sincerity of flag displays after 9/11 in Arab- and Muslim-American homes and neighborhoods.

- What do you consider a misuse of the flag?

- When, if ever, have you been provoked by misuse of the flag?

- Has the flag's presence ever made you feel uncomfortable? Why?

'The Star-Spangled Banner' as an American Symbol

America's national anthem, *The Star-Spangled Banner*, is partner to the flag itself. Hearing or singing the anthem often stirs emotion, just as the sight of Old Glory does. The rise of the American flag in the 1800s as a prominent symbol of national identity and a cherished icon correlated directly with the emergence of *The Star-Spangled Banner*. Francis Scott Key gave the flag new prominence when he asserted that "our flag was still there." The Star-Spangled Banner provided a renewed sense of patriotism and feelings of unity and pride.

Every schoolchild learns that Francis Scott Key penned the lyrics when he witnessed the British shelling of Fort McHenry during the War of 1812. But not every schoolchild knows that Key was a slave owner. As described in *Liberty and Freedom*, Key was born into a wealthy aristocratic family in old Maryland. The family itself owned slaves in five counties.

The Star-Spangled Banner wasn't the official national anthem until 1931. Earlier anthems were *Hail, Columbia* (now used when the vice president makes an official entrance) and *My Country, 'Tis of Thee*. National Anthem Day is March 3, though this observance is so obscure that it doesn't even show up in Google's U.S. holiday calendar. National Anthem Day marks the day in 1931 when President Hoover signed into law the resolution adopting *The Star-Spangled Banner* as the official anthem of the United States of America.

Key originally called his poem *The Defense of Fort McHenry*, which, one must admit, is not too catchy. But the tune itself caught on. Key recycled the melody of *To Anacreon in Heaven*, setting his words to match this well-known piece. This was the official song of an 18th century London gentlemen's club, called the Anacreontic Society. It was a club for professional men in law, medicine, business, trades and others who were devoted to musical performances and good food and drink. They named their club after the ancient Greek poet Anacreon, whose poems celebrated wine and women.

Some historians believed that Key's brother-in-law suggested the association of Key's lyrics with this melody. But an article published many years ago in *The Musical Quarterly* set the record straight: Key knew the tune before writing his lyrics. More than thirty popular songs had used the *Anacreon* melody from 1797 until the time when Key put pen to paper. One of these, *Adams and Liberty*, a celebration of our second president, was extremely popular. And, Key himself is said to be the author of a song set to the same melody nine years prior to the bombardment of Fort McHenry. This piece, called *My Bottle*, says the "magic draught" inspires writing and remedies the pains of domestic strife, creditors and physical aches.

Some say *The Star-Spangled Banner* is descended from a drinking song, noting the celebration of wine in *To Anacreon in Heaven*. No doubt some renditions of the recycled tune were drinking songs. *My Bottle* certainly seems to be one.

The lyrics of *The Anacreontic Song* are available online. Of course, the origin of this song is mostly forgotten, along with most of the recycled versions. The national anthem remains and stands as perhaps the most patriotic song in America.

"I was leading a 28-day tour of Europe for high school students. On the 4th of July we found ourselves in Paris. The father of one of the students had lived and worked in Paris and encouraged us to visit the U.S. Embassy, especially on the 4th as they used to throw a party for Americans. We walked to the Embassy only to find it closed. The Guards informed us that the 'party' had been the night before. The young people pleaded with the guards to just open the gate and let us stand on U.S. property on the 4th of July. Reluctantly they agreed, but we could stay for just a few minutes. Standing just inside the gate, one of the young women started singing the Star Spangled Banner. Spontaneously, everyone joined in. When we reached 'the home of the brave,' everyone had tears in their eyes, including the guards! It was one of the most powerful experiences of patriotism I have experienced."

Posted by Beth Miller on OurValues.org.

The Star-Spangled Banner is played for official government and military occasions. U.S. military bases play the national anthem at the beginning and end of each day. Those who remember the days before 24/7 media will recall when television and radio stations played it when they went off the air each evening. *The Star-Spangled Banner* is played during the Olympic Games when a U.S. athlete wins a gold medal. It is typically played at most major sporting events in the United States. It is considered an honor to be chosen to perform the national anthem for these occasions. The crowd stands, hands are placed over the heart, members of the military offer salutes, and many join in the singing.

One of the first controversial renditions of the national anthem happened in Detroit in 1968 at Tiger Stadium before game five of the World Series. Twenty-three-year-old Jose

Feliciano, a blind Puerto Rican musician, offered a slow, bluesy version of the national anthem. It damaged his career. His untraditional acoustic version was considered by many as sacrilegious, disrespectful and downright unpatriotic at a time when the country was torn apart by the Vietnam War.

Other memorable and controversial interpretations include those by Jimi Hendrix, Marvin Gaye and Whitney Houston. Christine Aguilera is remembered for forgetting the words when she sang at Super Bowl XLV in 2011. A video went viral of 13-year-old Natalie Gilbert who also forgot the words when she sang the anthem at a Portland Trailblazers home game. Head coach Mo Cheeks rushed to her side, helping Natalie finish the song. The crowd sang with them and the pair got a standing ovation.

No rendition of the anthem generated more ill will than when Roseanne Barr screeched an off-key version in 1990 at the opening of a San Diego Padres baseball game. She was booed and responded by spitting and grabbing her crotch. Then-president George H.W. Bush called it "disgraceful."

- When *The Star-Spangled Banner* is played, do you sing along?

- What feelings does *The Star-Spangled Banner* arouse when you hear it—or sing it?

- What is your response when someone changes the musical style of the national anthem?

- Do feel differently about Francis Scott Key, now that you know he was a slave owner?

Patriotic Holidays and Events

National celebrations can also provide a sense of unity and the feeling of patriotism. Our nation especially rallies around American values on the Independence Day weekend. The Fourth of July parades, speeches, flag-waving, fireworks, barbecues and other customary events combine symbols of America with the feeling of a nationally shared experience.

It's not the same for everyone. For some, the Fourth is nothing more than a summer festival. For others, it takes on solemn patriotic tones. In one family I know, the patriarch is a Russian immigrant and he marks the holiday each year by reading aloud the Declaration of Independence.

On Memorial Day, the nation pauses to pay homage to American servicemen and servicewomen killed in the line of duty. In towns across America, local scout troops and high school bands join veterans to march down Main Street. Ceremonies follow. Often, wreaths are laid, speeches given and a 21-gun salute marks the occasion.

The generally accepted history of Memorial Day is changing right before our eyes. Most history books don't have the updated version yet, which dates to a 2002 book, *Race and Reunion* by historian David W. Blight.

Do you know this updated—actually, restored—version of our history? Do you know when our first Memorial Day took place? Why? Where? Who honored which fallen soldiers?

I didn't and most Americans didn't throughout the entire 20th century. The memory had been lost in time. That is until Blight, professor of American history at Yale University, recovered the memory for all of us.

Blight's discovery is a remarkable piece of historical detective work. The first clue he found actually was something written by a Union soldier about the first Decoration Day. This important puzzle piece was not cataloged in the archives so its existence was unknown for more than 140 years. With this clue in hand, Blight went digging. He finally found the 1865 article in the Charleston newspaper headlined, "Martyrs of the Race Course" and then he documented this entire missing chapter in our history.

Here's a summary of what happened: The first Memorial Day took place in April 1865, soon after the end of the Civil War. The setting was Charleston. And it was led by former slaves to honor hundreds of Union soldiers who had died in a Confederate prison camp. The soldiers were not given proper burials, so the former slaves disinterred them and reburied them properly. Then, a full-day event took place, honoring the fallen soldiers. More than 10,000 former slaves participated. Today, we honor veterans and soldiers who fought and died mostly in foreign lands. The first Memorial Day, however, was to honor soldiers who died in their own country, fighting to reunite a divided land.

- What does this story of the first Memorial Day mean to you?

- What do you think about Blight's restoration of the record?

- How (or why) do you think we could have "lost" this history for over 100 years?

Patriotic holidays are widely observed American celebrations. But events, such as the Olympics, can also trigger the spirit of patriotism. In the summer of 2008, my young son and I were watching the semifinal match in women's beach volleyball: Brazil's Talita and Renata versus United States' Walsh and May-Trenor. After the American duo scored, he said, "That's good, right? Those are the Americans, right? We're supposed to cheer for them, right?"

The interrogative "right" turned statements into questions—questions about the link between Olympic competition and love of country. We had an interesting discussion about the good feelings that arise when one's countrymen and countrywomen win, and the importance of celebrating athletic achievement regardless of place or politics.

"Where we love is home—home that our feet may leave, but not our hearts."

Oliver Wendell Holmes

For many, the Olympics are all about national pride. The Olympic Movement states as one of the purposes of this world competition: "help to build a better world through sport practiced in a spirit of peace, excellence, friendship and respect." Yet, the medal count for the country is announced and celebrated daily. Indeed, the desire by the American media to highlight American achievements in the games has created a bit of a tricky situation. American Olympians came out on top in the medal count in 2008 but only if the total number was considered: gold, silver and bronze combined. China reigned first if the number of gold medals was used for ranking. It can be illuminating to peruse the various media and see which system they use to report the competition of "most medals."

The Olympics is about geopolitics, too. In 1980, then-President Jimmy Carter boycotted the Moscow Summer Olympics in protest of the Soviet Union's invasion of Afghanistan the year before. Many other nations followed America's lead. And symbols played a role: the green-gold-red flag of Los Angeles, California, was raised at the end of the 1980 Olympics, instead of Old Glory, to represent the city (but not the country) that would host the 1984 summer games.

- How do you respond to Olympics coverage?

- How would you have answered my son's questions?

- Do you feel proud when a U.S. Olympian wins a medal?

- Do you think the Olympics serve national interests more than the interests of a global community?

Summarizing Symbolic Patriotism

Patriotism is alive and well in America. Seeing the American flag or hearing the national anthem stirs positive emotions in the vast majority of Americans, uniting us despite our differences in many other aspects of life. Symbols of patriotism evoke a variety of feelings and sentiments. American symbols can also stir negative emotions. The flag and anthem may remind us of unjust wars, racism, and all the ways in which we don't live up to American ideals.

An important function of American symbols, such as the flag or national anthem, is providing a sense of identity and unity. These symbols help us feel connected to fellow members of a national community. They remind us of our common bonds and the ideals of our nation. Symbols are especially potent in America because we are not like most nations—where the feeling of belonging to a "people" comes from common ancestry, history, customs, language and religion. In America, the feeling of belonging comes from shared values and ideals. Patriotic symbols, celebrations, and rituals express a shared sense of being American.

Online resources to explore the topic of symbolic patriotism are available at UnitedAmericaBook.com and include materials for group activities and online reader discussions.

CHAPTER 3

Freedom

"**GIVE ME LIBERTY** or give me death!" Patrick Henry's fiery declaration is one of the best-known lines in American history. This proclamation came from an impassioned speech he made to the Virginia Convention in 1775. His oratory helped persuade the Virginia House of Burgesses (an elected governing body) to raise a militia for the War of Independence.

"Gentlemen may cry, Peace, Peace but there is no peace. The war is actually begun! ... Our brethren are already in the field! Why stand we here idle? Is life so dear, or peace so sweet, as to be purchased at the price of chains and slavery? Forbid it, Almighty God! I know not what course others may take; but as for me, give me liberty or give me death!"

Patrick Henry

My national surveys show that freedom continues to be a Core American Value. In this chapter, we will explore the many meanings of freedom and how our concepts were shaped by America's Founding Fathers. As we attempt to define freedom, I invite you to join in this process and to contemplate the meaning of freedom and how it is currently expressed and put to the test in America.

Specific examples from American life are offered to stimulate thinking about how the value of freedom influences your choices and attitudes. How do we resolve issues when personal freedoms infringe on the freedom of others? How do we ensure freedom for everyone in America? When and where is freedom put to the test? This chapter will raise these questions and more as you consider freedom as a Core American Value.

Defining Freedom and Liberty

Americans hold tenaciously to the principles of liberty and freedom. Countless Americans have given their lives for these ideals. But what did Patrick Henry mean by liberty? Was it the same as freedom?

Freedom and liberty are often used interchangeably. They are related but distinct concepts. Liberty refers to freedom from restraint. Natural liberty means being left alone to do what one wants, without restraint or outside interference. The rattlesnake ("Don't tread on me") was a symbol of natural liberty in colonial America, notes historian David Hackett

Fischer. Centuries later, the American Tea Party movement adopted the rattlesnake and motto as its symbol.

"Order without liberty and liberty without order are equally destructive."

Theodore Roosevelt

Liberty and freedom are ancient concepts, but English is the only language that uses both of them in common speech, says Fischer. Originally, liberty (*libertas* in Latin) meant the absence of restraints or bonds. Today, liberty also means independence and separation. Freedom (which has the same root as friend) referred to the rights, duties, and protections of belonging to a free tribe. Freedom, in other words, is really about connection. Liberty and freedom—separation and connection—are ideas that co-exist but sometimes conflict with one another, as we shall see in this chapter.

"If the freedom of speech is taken away then dumb and silent we may be led, like sheep to the slaughter."

George Washington

- When have you exercised your freedom to join a group— or to leave a group and "do your own thing"?

- How would you describe the difference between liberty and freedom?

- Is one more important to you than the other? Why?

Origins of American Concepts of Freedom

Our ideas about freedom continue to evolve and adapt, and in recent years, we've heard many voices calling us to return to the words of our Founding Fathers. It is a challenge to truly comprehend the intent of the writers of the nation's "freedom documents"—the Declaration of Independence, Constitution, Bill of Rights—and then apply our interpretations to current times.

For one answer, let's go to the source: Thomas Jefferson, the author of what historian Joseph J. Ellis calls "the best known 58 words in American history." These words are: "We hold these truths to be self-evident; that all men are created equal; that they are endowed by their creator with certain [inherent and] inalienable Rights; that among these are life, liberty & the pursuit of happiness; that to secure these rights, governments are instituted among men, deriving just powers from the consent of the governed."

Jefferson wrote these words (and drafted the rest of the Declaration of Independence) working alone in the summer of 1776. The writing is considered by many to be a "quasi-religious episode in American history," writes Ellis in his biography of Jefferson. It was a "moment when, at least according to the most romantic explanations, a solitary Jefferson was allowed a glimpse of the eternal truths and then offered the literary inspiration to inscribe them on the American soul."

Jefferson had a theory about the origin of American values—about those eternal truths he had glimpsed in the summer of 1776. He revealed it in earlier writings. Jefferson believed that American values went back to the Saxon world before the Norman Conquest in 1066, and before that to the forests of Germany. According to Ellis, Jefferson imagined the Saxons and ancient Germans to be "people who lived freely and harmoniously, without kings or lords to rule over them, working and owning their land as sovereign agents."

Jefferson saw America as a rebirth of these ancient values, re-established in a new world where people would live in harmony without monarchs or big government. The pristine past of Jefferson's imagination might not have been so harmonious in reality, but Ellis says it appealed to Jefferson's way of thinking. This imagined past "gave narrative shape to his fondest imaginings and to utopian expectations with deep roots in his personality."

The Jeffersonian principles of limited government and individual freedom live today—some say to ill effect. As Ellis puts it, "American political discourse is phrased in Jeffersonian terms as a conversation about sovereign individuals who only grudgingly and in special circumstances are prepared to compromise that sovereignty for larger social purposes."

Times have changed since the agrarian society of Jefferson's day. America is a lot larger and more complex. And I'm sure Jefferson's slaves would have had a thing or two to say about living in "perfect harmony." But the romance of Jefferson's ideals still appeals to most Americans.

"I had crossed the line. I was free; but there was no one to welcome me to the land of freedom. I was a stranger in a strange land."

Harriet Tubman

Liberty and freedom are as important today as they were when the freedom documents were written. But the concepts of liberty and freedom compete with one another. You just read about Jefferson's strongly held ideals concerning freedom. In spite of these ideals, Jefferson also believed he was at liberty to enslave those of another race. And, as bizarre as it sounds today, in the run up to the Civil War, Southern planters argued that it was "their absolute liberty to keep a slave," says Fischer. American history records many other examples of liberty in conflict with freedom.

- Do liberty and freedom mean the same thing to you?

- What or who has influenced your ideas about freedom?

- In your family, what are the "rules" or guidelines that dictate how individual liberty is limited in order for your family to function?

What do Americans Mean by Freedom?

In his 1941 State of the Union Address, President Franklin D. Roosevelt outlined what he called "four essential human freedoms." These were not just American freedoms, but aspirations for the entire world.

> "The first is freedom of speech and expression—everywhere in the world.
> "The second is freedom of every person to worship God in his own way—everywhere in the world.
> "The third is freedom from want—which, translated into world terms, means economic understandings which will secure to every nation a healthy peacetime life for its inhabitants-everywhere in the world.
> "The fourth is freedom from fear—which, translated into world terms, means a world-wide reduction of armaments to such a point and in such a thorough fashion that no nation will be in a position to commit an act of physical aggression against any neighbor—anywhere in the world."

In the sixty-plus years since Roosevelt delivered this address, the gap between these ideals and reality remains wide, both here and abroad. In America, more progress has been made on the first two than the last two. Today, for example, economic inequality is at an all-time high, a challenge to the ideal of freedom from want. But I name these four freedoms not to judge them but to use them as illustrations of the many meanings of freedom.

> *"Nothing is more wonderful than the art of being free, but nothing is harder to learn than how to use freedom."*
>
> **Alexis de Tocqueville**

What does freedom mean to you? I asked my young son that question. "To be away from my parents and not have to follow their rules," he answered. Ah, I thought, freedom from the tyranny of oppression and arbitrary rule! He's starting to get the idea.

For most Americans, freedom is not an abstraction. It is a set of values that we learn early in life (like my son's example). The meaning of freedom is part of our cultural DNA, transmitted from generation to generation. Yet, like biological DNA, it mutates, recombines, and is remade into something new with each generation. But it remains a core value that we easily recognize.

> *"For to be free is not merely to cast off one's chains, but to live in a way that respects and enhances the freedom of others."*
>
> **Nelson Mandela**

To explore the meanings of freedom, in my surveys I asked about four different definitions of freedom. These were presented as statements, and respondents were asked to indicate the extent to which they agreed or disagreed with a statement. Here are the four statements. To what extent do you agree or disagree with each one?

1. Freedom is being left alone to do what I want.
2. Freedom is having a government that doesn't interfere in my life.

3. Freedom is having the right to participate in politics and elections.
4. Freedom is being able to express unpopular ideas without fearing for my safety.

If you are like most Americans, you don't feel the same about all of these definitions of freedom. Is freedom being left alone to do what you want? The majority of Americans (61 percent) don't agree with this definition, I found. Reasoning and experience tell us that the idea of freedom without limitations is absurd. This is true not only for individuals but also governments; no rights are absolute and without restraint.

"Rightful liberty is unobstructed action according to our will within limits drawn around us by the equal rights of others."

Thomas Jefferson

How about not having a government that interferes in your life? Is that the freedom we value? Half of Americans agree with this definition of freedom and about one-third disagree. The rest (about 15 percent) neither agree nor disagree.

If you agree with the third and fourth statements, however, then you have identified the core value of freedom that unites nearly all Americans—more than 90 percent agree with these third and fourth statements.

Thomas Jefferson said, "The business of government is to govern." For everyone to have freedom, there must be boundaries and limits set by those elected to govern. Jefferson believed in freedom from despotic oppression, but freedom within the confines of law and order for the good of all. Yet many Americans feel the government has gone too far. A 2013 poll by the Pew Research Center shows that 53 percent of Americans see the federal government as a threat to personal rights and freedoms. This is the first time since Pew started asking about this issue in 1995 that a majority felt this way.

"You have freedom when you're easy in your harness."

Robert Frost

Is freedom having the right to participate in politics and elections? Almost all Americans say yes—98 percent agree with this definition of freedom. How about the fourth definition of freedom? Here, too, we see widespread agreement. More than nine of ten Americans (92 percent) agree with this definition. These two definitions of freedom are closely related to another core value: Critical Patriotism. (See Chapter 10 for a discussion of this Core American Value.)

"My definition of a free society is a society where it is safe to be unpopular."

Adlai Stevenson

"When I think of freedom in America, I think freedom is one of our hopeful and courageous ideals. I think of Dietrich Bonheoffer: He talks about being "free from" to be "free for." Part of our idealized American vision is that we can be free to be ourselves, free to explore opportunities, free to get curious and free to really begin the experiment of what citizenship and community are all about. Freedom is one of the ideals that has made America great and potentially can again. Freedom is one of the valiant ideals of American self-identity."

Posted by Canon Marianne Borg on OurValues.org, August 18, 2010.

- What does freedom mean to you?

- How much progress have we made on Roosevelt's Four Freedoms?

- For you, which is the most important definition of freedom listed above?

- Which definition is the least important?

> *"I am deeply appreciative of freedom of speech, freedom of movement and all those good things. There are wonderful things about our freedoms. But when our concept of freedom becomes freedom for a few and not a lot of freedom for others, then we've got a problem. Liberty and justice go together. Without justice, then people are imprisoned in many ways. And of course liberty and justice are right there together in the Pledge of Allegiance."*
>
> **Posted by Marcus Borg on OurValues.org, August 17, 2010.**

To round out our consideration of the core value of freedom, let's examine the idea of freedom in three very different areas of American life: our car culture, the right to work and populist movements like the Tea Party.

America's Car Culture and Freedom

Does your car set you free? Is driving an expression of freedom?

The car was always more than mere transportation. The car has always been associated with freedom and independence, notes Cotten Seiler in *Republic of Drivers*. Seiler says that the act of driving has even monopolized our conceptions of freedom and liberty. Consider, for example, the first image that came to Ronald Reagan's mind when David Frost asked what "freedom" meant to him. Writing in *The Atlantic*, Kathleen Kennedy Townsend recalls Reagan's reply: "He described driving up the Pacific Coast Highway in a convertible with the wind blowing through his hair. His first image was a man doing his own thing, alone."

Terry Gallagher, a popular guest author on my blog, Our-Values.org, wrote a column about cars and freedom—and presents a different view:

> *Remember that commercial from a decade ago: 'It's not just your car; it's your freedom'? The General Motors slogan really tugged on those old stereotypes of hitting the open road with the wind in your hair and no clouds on the horizon.*
>
> *That's really hooey, isn't it? It's a completely false view of freedom—when it comes with six years of payments, plus insurance, maintenance, storage and gas prices what they are. But the idea that owning a car makes you free might be one of the reasons we see so many terrible drivers out there. For many people, being behind the wheel is their only chance to let it all hang out. Your car is one of the very few places you can smoke anymore, so why not throw butts out the window?*

Some values trump freedom. As Terry puts it, *"Values like driving safely and yielding courteously. Values like recognizing that you're not the only driver on this freeway. After all, it's not your freedom. It's just a car."*

"As a teenager driving west on I-80 with two friends about to begin our freshman year at BYU, we sailed across the barren landscape of Wyoming. I felt the thrill of independence and freedom like never before. Of course that all changed as the hard work of classes, jobs and life, overwhelmed that wide-open landscape. Perhaps cars have a way to help us connect to those simple memories: First dates, driving home with a new infant in a shiny car seat, helping your mother into the freshly washed car at your father's funeral, picking up your teen after work and then talking the whole way home."

Posted by SusanM on OurValues.org, July 18, 2012.

- Do you think of your car as freedom? Why or why not?

- What would you say is a symbol of freedom for you personally?

- As a culture, what do you see as symbols of freedom?

Right to Work and Freedom

"Right to work" is a loaded phrase. It implies that our freedom to work and earn a living has somehow been denied. But "right to work" is wordplay meant to tap the emotions we have around cherished ideas of freedom and liberty. Many people have a positive reaction to the phrase—until they understand what it really means.

In states without right-to-work laws, a labor union can require all employees to join the union and pay union dues, whether they want to or not. Right-to-work states, however, remove this condition of employment. An employee is free to join the union and pay dues or not join and not pay union dues. The union can't exclude non-union workers.

Right-to-work creates a situation in which an employee can benefit from collective bargaining without paying a share of the costs to the union. Business favors right-to-work because it weakens the union. A 2011 study by the Economic Policy Institute (which is partly funded by organized labor) found that wages were lower in right-to-work states than in states without these laws. The rates of employer-sponsored health insurance and pensions were also lower. However, the employment rate was higher in right-to-work states.

About half of all states have right-to-work laws. Most of these are in the south and west. But in 2012, both Michigan and Indiana became right-to-work states. The passage of the law in Michigan was a particular blow to organized labor because of the central role Michigan played in the history of industrial unions.

In the same year that Michigan and Indiana passed right-to-work laws, the U.S. Supreme Court made a decision that weakens public-sector unions. Terry Gallagher, a popular guest columnist on OurValues.org, wrote about this ruling and how it may represent a broader trend—opting out of our duties and responsibilities. Here's Terry's argument:

> *Could the new 'opt out' ruling cripple unions? The U.S. Supreme Court handed down a decision criticized by many as an overreaching assault on the rights of working people. This ruling moved in the direction of crippling unions, critics argued. Defenders of this ruling argued that it was an essential re-affirmation of individuals' rights. (The case was Knox v. Service Employees International Union.)*

The case revolved around one of the basic issues in an 'agency shop,' where all workers in a unit, organized by a union, pay the equivalent of union dues to cover the costs of negotiating and defending their contracts, whether they choose to be members of the union or not. In this case, all the workers covered by the contract also were assessed a fee to cover political advocacy—over and above the costs of representation—with the option of opting out of that fee. In the end, however, many workers found themselves contributing to political campaigns they didn't support.

The high court ruled 7-2 'that when a union imposes a special assessment not previously disclosed, not only must the union provide a new notice but non-members must affirmatively 'opt-in' to paying the assessment, contrary to the long-standing 'opt-out' rule in the union dues context'.

"That's the same court that insists corporations are people and one dollar is one vote. Democracy in the USA "a noble experiment," now failed."

Posted on OurValues.org by unattributed.

"Just another nail in the 40-year effort to put unions in a coffin ... You know, unions? The people and groups that built the middle class, fought and died for us to be able to come together and collectively bargain, fought for weekends, 8 hr. workdays, holidays, OSHA, child labor laws, suffrage?"

Posted on OurValues.org by unattributed.

Terry continues:

> *Two justices traditionally considered part of the court's liberal wing, Sotomayer and Ginsburg, joined the majority. They shared in their own separate opinion on the case. Overall, this strong 7-2 majority looked like a slam-dunk for individual liberty, the notion that no one should be compelled to support a cause or candidate they didn't like.*
>
> *On the other hand, many people saw the decision as the thin end of a wedge aimed at destroying the ability of workers to come together to fight for their common interests.*
>
> *Next was the Supreme Court decision limiting union flexibility in political activism—centering on employees who want to opt out on various political causes.*

There's a clear pattern in all these court decisions and rulings, says Gallagher, and it indicates a trend in our society to get away and opt out of our responsibilities and duties.

"While the overall trend of 'opting out' does seem a little overly individualistic, as one of those individuals, I know I opt out as much as possible, just to prevent my information being disseminated."

Posted by Dmitri on OurValues.org, July 20, 2012.

- What emotions do you feel when you hear "right to work"?

- Does a right-to-work law mean more freedom—or less?

- Do you think the freedom to "opt out" could cripple unions?

- Are we "opting out" too much in our lives?

The Tea Party and Freedom

What does the rise of the Tea Party in 2009 tell us about freedom? This political movement is a mix of conservative, libertarian and populist principles. At the heart of the movement is the ideal of America as a nation of autonomous individuals and limited government. Big Government is Big Brother stripping away our freedoms one by one. For Tea Partiers, bailouts and healthcare reform are evidence that government is too big and out of control. The movement advocates permanent tax cuts, reduced government spending, a balanced budget and strict adherence to the U.S. Constitution.

This movement takes its name and symbols from America's iconic past, attempting to evoke the same spirit of liberty, legitimacy of cause and revolutionary fervor. The modern Tea Party quickly adopted the colonial symbol of natural liberty mentioned above: the rattlesnake and motto "Don't tread on me." The movement's values are closer to the concept of liberty than freedom, emphasizing the absence of restraints and bonds.

How "American" is the Tea Party, really? One way to answer this question is to compare the Tea Party in the 21st century to the original Tea Party of 1773.

The original Boston Tea Party was a response to many actions, some arbitrary and punitive, by what was increasingly seen as a foreign power and occupying force—Britain. It followed, for example, the quartering of British soldiers, the so-called Townshend Acts meant to raise revenue and punish the colonists and the Boston Massacre. After the massacre, the British removed troops from Boston and repealed the Townshend Acts. What was left was the tea tax. It was the straw that broke the camel's back.

The protesters dressed as Indians because the indigenous peoples were symbols of freedom in colonial times. The dumping of East Indian tea into the Boston harbor was carefully done. Protesters were careful to avoid violating other laws. The tea tax was symbolic; so was the protest.

Fast forward about 250 years. Now, we have Tea Partiers masquerading as the original Tea Party. Their quarrel is not with an occupying foreign power, one that enacts taxation without representation. Rather, it is the latest recycling of a particular vision of America: the ideals of limited government and individual liberty.

Whether we like the Tea Party or not, we have to recognize that it draws its power from these Jeffersonian principles. The Tea Party's policy prescriptions may be unrealistic, naïve, or even harmful, but they resonate: small government "feels right" to many Americans and big government "feels wrong." As *Boiling Mad* author Kate Zernike says in the prologue to her book, "The Tea Party movement went to the heart of conflicts that had bedeviled Americans for more than two hundred years and reflected anxieties that Americans had been expressing for generations." I think she's right.

The Tea Party may seem extreme to most Democrats or moderate Republicans, but they cannot compare to the extremism of the anti-government "Hutaree" or "Guardians of the Free Republics."

These radical groups were not part of my working vocabulary until their activities thrust them into the national arena, capturing media attention. The FBI arrested members of the Hutaree, a radical Christian militia group in Michigan, for allegedly planning to murder a police officer and then detonate a bomb at the funeral, thus killing other officers in attendance. The Guardians—part of the sovereign citizen movement—declared a vow of nonviolence, but sent letters to state governors, telling them to step down or be taken down.

> *"I'm afraid for too many Americans, freedom primarily means radical individualism. I want to emphasize in my definition of freedom: freedom from fear. I think we live in a time in which powerful agents and voices in our culture cultivate fear in politics and in religion."*
>
> **Posted by Marcus Borg on OurValues.org, August 17, 2010.**

Why do these extremist groups exist? It's too easy to dismiss them as a bunch of right-wing nuts.

In a way, they are American—just too much American—and perhaps, at the same time, they're not American at all. The principles they stand for—liberty, limited government, self-reliance, and patriotism—are American values. It's just that they've taken them to the utmost extreme, and they have not balanced these values with others that are part of America's Core Values: respect for others, kindness, justice and fairness.

> *"From the equality of rights springs identity of our highest interests; you cannot subvert your neighbor's rights without striking a dangerous blow at your own."*
>
> **Carl Schurz**

American values are a two-edged sword. They are sources of strength and causes of problems. Liberty without restraint is blind to the welfare of the whole. When extremist groups cry "liberty" and threaten the lives of other Americans because they hold opposing views, something is terribly wrong.

- What's your opinion of the Tea Party?

- Do you resonate with any ideas from the Tea Party movement?

- What Tea Party ideas seem unrealistic or harmful?

- Should extremist groups like Hutaree have the freedom to exist in America? Why or why not?

Summarizing Freedom

From the early days of the Republic until the present, freedom continues to be a Core American Value. Our understanding of freedom is shaped significantly by the writings and philosophies of the nation's Founding Fathers. However, our concepts of freedom have changed over time.

Freedom is multi-faceted, subject to debate, ever interpreted, changeable across time and situations—and yet, like cultural DNA that gets recombined and made into something new with each generation, it remains a core value that we easily recognize. How we understand the meaning and practice of freedom will continue to evolve.

Freedom is often "put to the test"—not only in judicial decisions but in our daily lives. When taken to the extreme, we realize that freedom can be misused. Americans will never abandon freedom as a core value. But we will continue to debate the many meanings of freedom and find new expressions of what it means to be a free people.

Online resources to explore the topic of freedom are available at UnitedAmericaBook.com and include materials for group activities and online reader discussions.

CHAPTER 4

Security

ONE OF AMERICA'S iconic images of security comes from cartoonist Charles Schulz. Lucy's little brother, Linus, is rarely depicted without sucking his thumb and clutching his "security blanket." Family mem-bers try to pry it away from him, and Linus tries many times to give it up, but all to no avail. One time, Lucy used his blanket as a dishtowel to dry the dishes. "We now have very secure dishes," Linus said. After his grandmother takes the blanket and gives him a dollar for it, we see Linus sucking his thumb and holding the bill to his face. "I don't feel very secure," he tells Charlie Brown.

I don't mean to trivialize security by using this example, but to emphasize that the need for security is part of the human condition. Safety and security are at the foundation of our human needs.

Security means many things. Security can mean protection from harm, freedom from dangers and threats, enough food and proper shelter. People install elaborate security systems to protect their homes and families. Financial security is important to almost all Americans. Security can mean psychological safety in the workplace (freedom to speak up) and emotional safety in our personal relationships.

In this chapter, our focus is national security. Keeping the nation safe and secure is now a major priority—perhaps an obsession. National security is one of the Ten Core American Values. We will take a close look at our desire for national security and how it shapes national policies and personal attitudes. We'll look at the reasons why there haven't been additional terror attacks by external forces on U.S. soil since 9/11 and the creation of new Homeland Security agencies. We'll consider our defense budget and the costs of the wars in Iraq and Afghanistan. We'll also look at fears of Muslim "radicalization" and homegrown terrorism. Immigration is our last topic.

Defining National Security

Security refers to concerns for safety of self, family, and others, as well as the general stability and harmony of society. National security refers to the protection of self, family, and country from internal and external threats, real or perceived.

It is fascinating to look at the Preamble to the U.S. Constitution through the lens of national security. Here is what it says:

"We the people of the United States, in order to form a more perfect union, establish justice, insure domestic tranquility, provide for the common defense, promote the general welfare, and secure the blessings of liberty to ourselves and our posterity, do ordain and establish this Constitution for the United States of America."

The words "domestic tranquility," "common defense," "general welfare," and securing liberty elevate the importance of national security for the nation.

National security is important to the vast majority of Americans. Eight-five percent of Americans agree that "The protection of the United States from both internal and external threats is a major concern for me." How far are you willing to go to ensure national security? Are you willing to trade the core value of freedom for the core value of security? Many Americans are willing to make this trade, giving up individual freedoms to protect the country. In a survey my team and I conducted a few years after 9/11, we learned that the majority of the general population (55 percent) in the greater Detroit region was willing to give up civil liberties to curb terrorism. But what surprised us was that many Arab-Americans (47 percent) also would be willing to give up personal freedoms to curb terrorism.

"Security commands moral precedence ... Not to be killed, maimed, or tortured is the most basic of human rights. Significantly, life precedes both liberty and the pursuit of happiness in the Declaration of Independence's lineup of the purposes for which government is instituted."

Amitai Etzioni, *Security First.*

> *"If you want total security, go to prison. There you're fed, clothed, given medical care and so on. The only thing lacking ... is freedom."*
>
> **Dwight D. Eisenhower**

Our society has undergone a lot of changes since 9/11, meant to protect the nation against threats to our national security. I'm not sure if I feel safer or not. I certainly feel more inconvenienced, especially every time I go through airport security, shoes off, pockets empty, and nothing in my hand except a boarding pass.

- What is the first image that comes to mind when you hear the word "security"?

- What phrases or words emerge when you hear the word "security"?

- Is protecting the United States from both internal and external threats a major concern for you?

Why No Attacks on U.S. Soil Since 9/11?

The tenth anniversary of the terror attacks on September 11, 2001, saw a media flood of articles, footage and questions on national security. In the buildup to the anniversary, the news covered every possible theme, detail and angle. It was an emotional and heart-wrenching week as many, especially those who had lost family members, relived the tragedy. We saw a strengthening of security in public places, transportation systems, power plants, major events and other sites that week. Al-Qaida cited the tenth observance of 9/11 as a possible occasion to strike again. Fortunately, no acts of terrorism occurred on American soil that week.

Since the tenth anniversary of 9/11, we've experienced the tragedies of mass shootings of children and the Boston bombing. Internal threats continue to loom. Why haven't we had another major terror attack on American soil by external forces? Is it because our government's deterrence and detection methods are so good? Are airport security checks the reason? Perhaps the wars in Iraq and Afghanistan helped to prevent a new attack? Or is it just plain dumb luck?

We don't really know the answer, of course. It could be all of these reasons, or some other factors we haven't considered. Whatever the facts are, it's instructive to consider what Americans believe about this question. Beliefs can shape our decisions and actions more than facts do.

"I don't think it would be as easy to execute a major attack like 9/11 with the precautions that the government has taken since the attack."

Posted on OurValues.org by unattributed.

Just about everyone has an opinion about why we haven't seen another attack, according to a 2011 survey by the Pew Research Center. Here are a few of the results:

- Effective Precautions: Four of ten (43 percent) believe we haven't had a major attack since 9/11 because the government is doing a good job protecting the nation.
- Luck: About a third say it's just because we've been lucky so far. Older Americans are even more likely to cite luck as the reason.
- Tough Target: About one in four young Americans (ages 18–29) like to think it's because America is a difficult target, but only one in ten older Americans (65+) agrees with this.
- Don't Know: Only 7 percent of Americans say they don't know why.

> *"I'm not sure why we haven't had another attack, so I guess I'm a part of that 7 percent."*
>
> **Posted by Emily T. on OurValues.org, September 7, 2011.**

Have the decade-long wars in Iraq and Afghanistan—so costly in life and resources—lessened the chances of another major attack? Most Americans say no. Only one in four thinks the chances of another attack are lower because of these wars, with little variation in opinion between Republicans and Democrats. More Americans believe the wars have increased, rather than decreased, the chances of another terrorist attack, though Republicans are less likely than Democrats or Independents to agree.

> *"I don't think the ongoing wars in Iraq and Afghanistan are decreasing the chance of another attack. It's probably just fueling the minds of radicals, giving them more reason to lash out against us."*
>
> **Posted by Emily T. on OurValues.org, September 7, 2011.**

We may disagree on why the United States has not experienced an act of terror on our soil but we all agree on the enormity of the tragedy. Not only were over 2,750 lives lost on that single day, more than 1,000 have died since 9/11 from related illnesses. Many first responders have been slowly dying as health problems persist. At least 20,000 ground zero workers are being treated for associated illnesses and the World Trade Center Health Program continues to monitor thousands more. The cost continues to be high.

> *"Our country is safer and our people are resilient."*
>
> **President Obama, recalling the events of 9/11.**

The events of 9/11 continue to shape America. The quest for national security continues to influence not only how we live our lives but also government policies, agendas, and agencies.

- Why do you think there hasn't been an attack on U.S. soil by external forces since 9/11?

- Do you worry that we will eventually have another attack?

- In what ways are you resilient?

Homeland Security Agencies

Let's look closer at some of the government agency changes that have taken place in America since 9/11. One of the first moves to address issues of national security was the creation of the September 11 Commission in 2002. This bipartisan group presented a 587-page guide to create an America that, in their words, would be "safer, stronger and wiser."

As a result of their recommendations, several new government agencies were created to strengthen national security. How familiar are you with them? Acronyms that did not exist before 9/11 are now part of our national security system: Transportation Security Administration (TSA), Director of National Intelligence (DNI), Department of Homeland Security (DHS), National Counterterrorism Center (NCTC), Common Vulnerabilities and Exposures (CVE), National Security Institute (NSI) and Immigration and Customs Enforcement (ICE). What's gone? Terrorist Threat Integration Center (TTIC), Immigration and Naturalization Service (INS) and more.

By now, Homeland Security has become a household word, but before 9/11 the phrase wasn't used much. Can you remember life before the TSA? The Transportation Security Administration was created soon after the attacks. Now, engaging with a TSA agent is routine for anyone flying on commercial airplanes. Securing the sky has become a priority, with the United States pouring more than $50 billion into aviation security.

In December 2004, TTIC (the Terrorist Threat Integration Center) was superseded by the NCTC, the National Counterterrorism Center. The mission of the NCTC was to bring together all the government intelligence and analyst organizations. The new National Intelligence Officer position was to coordinate all of it. Several directors have held this position, often referred to as the "most thankless job in Washington." Turf battles between agencies continue as the intelligence budget has more than doubled since 9/11.

The well-known INS (Immigration and Naturalization Service) was replaced in 2003 by three new bodies: U.S. Citizenship and Immigration Services (USCIS), Immigration and Customs Enforcement (ICE) and the U.S. Customs and Border Protection (CBP)—all within the newly created Department of Homeland Security (DHS).

Living in Michigan, I've had plenty of encounters with these new agencies, especially when we sail our old family sailboat into Canada. When we return to American waters, we've been grilled at length. We've even had our boat searched.

One organization you may not have heard of is the Privacy and Civil Liberties Oversight Board or PCLOB. The PCLOB was created in response to a recommendation of the 9/11 Commission that "there should be a board within the executive branch to oversee … the commitment the government makes to defend our civil liberties." It was to ensure the government did not go too far with the new terrorism-fighting powers provided by the Patriot Act. Congress, realizing the need to balance security and civil liberty, feared that aggressive intelligence collection might unduly infringe on Americans' rights. For more than seven years the PCLOB, created in 2004, had no staff and no office. The need for the PCLOB points to the constant tension of American values: security and freedom.

> *"Those who desire to give up freedom in order to gain security will not have, nor do they deserve, either one."*
>
> **Benjamin Franklin**

- Have you had any personal interaction with any of these agencies? What is your reaction?

- How do you feel national security has been strengthened as a result of these agencies?

- How much freedom are you willing to give up for more security?

War: Is it Worth the Cost?

The 9/11-decade was a rollercoaster for America and for perceptions of the United States around the world. Everyone can remember the sympathy, outreach and support that America received in the months after 9/11. I recall getting emails from friends and colleagues around the world, expressing concern, worry and support.

This global outpouring of positive emotions waned quickly as what became known as the Bush Doctrine unfolded and America took unilateral and preventive military actions. The Pew Global Attitudes Project detected a decline in positive opinions about the United States as early as 2002. Negative opinions reversed with the election of Barack Obama, and the "Obama Bump" lasted for some time. This upswing in public opinion about America did not occur in predominately Muslim countries, according to Pew.

What has been the cost of both the Iraq and Afghanistan wars? Are we more secure as a result of the wars? Have the wars strengthened national security? Will our experiences in Iraq and Afghanistan continue to shape foreign policy? Opinions vary.

> *"I have no doubt in my mind that this "war" will be viewed by historians as one of the great foreign policy disasters that the U.S. has engaged in. It was deployed on false pretenses with a drumbeat of military bravado and saber rattling under a misguided foreign policy that seemed to understand little or nothing about the region."*
>
> **Posted by Russ on OurValues.org, December 19, 2011.**

December 15, 2011, marked the official end of the war in Iraq. U.S. flags in Iraq were lowered and "cased" to protect and ship home. The last American troops pulled out of Iraq, and we were officially out of the war that started in March 2003.

> *"...we have lost in so many ways not yet fully counted."*
>
> **Posted by Bob Bruttell on OurValues.org, December 19, 2011.**

Was it worth it?

> *"No it wasn't worth it. We attacked a country that hadn't attacked us, found no WMD, and it actually ended up being Pakistan that was hiding Bin Laden."*
>
> **Posted by Big Deac on OurValues.org, December 19, 2011.**

The costs have been immense. In his December 17, 2011, weekly address, Obama summed up the human costs for Americans:

"For nearly nine years, our nation has been at war in Iraq. More than 1.5 million Americans have served there with honor, skill and bravery. Tens of thousands have been wounded. Military families have sacrificed greatly—none more so than the families of those nearly 4,500 Americans who made the ultimate sacrifice. All of them—our troops, veterans, and their families—will always have the thanks of a grateful nation."

The cost to U.S. veterans continues. Many did not lose their lives, but they lost limbs, eyesight, mental health, their families and their jobs. It is currently estimated that one veteran a day in the United States commits suicide.

"What has America gained? Security? Iraq NEVER posed a threat to America or Israel. An ally in the Middle East? Iraqis will be a long, long time forgetting the sisters, brothers, children, etc. that America slaughtered."

Posted by Ron on OurValues.org, December 20, 2011.

And there's also the human cost on the other side. More than 100,000 Iraqis lost their lives as well. Iraq is forever altered and its fate remains uncertain.

> "I fear America has a video game mentality. The delusion that we can wipe out the "bad guys." But the attack itself, in real life, creates more bad guys and real people wearing a prosthesis or unable to think straight. All the while the ideas that motivated the bad guys do not die on the battlefields. That work must be done politically among the people—all the people on all sides. The delusion is that somehow you can avoid the hard part: contesting the ideas."
>
> **Posted by Bob Bruttell on OurValues.org, December 19, 2011.**

And there's the financial cost of the war. In the long term, the costs to the U.S. may exceed $4 trillion to $6 trillion, according to estimates reported in 2013 by *Defense News*.

> "The United States will be dealing with the closed head injuries, the PTSDs, the missing limbs, and the distressed children left without a parent ... they will carry the karma of our generation into the next. The costs will be huge. You strike but you don't know the whole score for several generations."
>
> **Posted by Bob Bruttell on OurValues.org, December 19, 2011.**

- Do you feel safer (or less safe) because of the wars?

- Do you think the wars were worth it?

- What impact did the wars have on your life personally?

National Security and Defense Spending

One cannot talk about national security without referring to defense spending. National security is often thought of in the military sense.

How much do you think the U.S. spends on defense? How does it compare to the total world's defense spending?

Every year, the International Institute for Strategic Studies (IISS) publishes a report on defense spending. U.S. defense spending for 2011 is reported at $739.3 billion. After years of increasing expenditures, defense spending in the United States is starting to decline, in part due to planned budget cuts, in part due to the across-the-board cuts mandated by the sequester. In 2012, the United States spent $682 billion on defense, according to the Stockholm International Peace Research Institute (SIPRI) Yearbook 2013. This is about 39 percent of defense spending by all countries combined.

"The problem in defense is how far you can go without destroying from within what you are trying to defend from without."

Dwight D. Eisenhower

The United States continues to rank No. 1 in defense spending. Who are the other big ones in 2012? The next ten, in order, are China, Russia, United Kingdom, Japan, France, Saudi Arabia, India, Germany, Italy and Brazil. U.S. defense spending is greater than the combined defense budgets of these ten countries.

China is increasing its military spending, while the United States is decreasing its spending. Still, U.S. spending is more than four times greater than China's, according to the SIPRI Yearbook.

Is our military spending in line with actual and anticipated threats? Are we spending more than we should on defense?

In 2011, Senate Democrats proposed cuts to the military budget, following a 70 percent increase in spending from 2001 to 2010. These suggested cuts were termed "devastating" by many. Sens. John McCain and Lindsey Graham warned, "These cuts represent a threat to the national security interests of the United States." Buck McKeon, the U.S. Representative for California's 25th congressional district and chairman of the House Armed Services Committee vowed, "I will not be the Armed Services Committee chairman who presides over the crippling of our military." Leon Panetta, Department of Defense secretary, said he feared the plan would "invite aggression." McCain and Graham also predicted the cuts would mean America would experience a "swift decline as the world's leading military power." In 2013, Panetta said that the sequester (mandatory across-the board budget cuts) would be "a shameful and irresponsible act."

"If we desire to secure peace, it must be known that we are at all times ready for war."

George Washington

How do these arguments sound to you in light of the statistics about defense spending? Cuts to defense are often cast as doomsday scenarios for national security. Does defense spending really translate into national security?

- How familiar were you with the military spending statistics before reading this chapter?

- Do these figures make you feel more secure? Why or why not?

- Why is defense spending an untouchable "sacred cow" in America?

Congressional Hearings on the 'Radicalization' of Muslims in America

U.S. Rep. Peter King was chairman of the House Homeland Security Committee in 2011. He headed up hearings on the "radicalization" of Muslims in the United States. These hearings played to fears that Al-Qaeda was stirring up homegrown terrorism in the United States.

"It was found that before WWII, few Germans were Nazis, and most didn't even like Hitler, but through apathy, they lost control of their country. This could happen here if we are not careful."

Posted by Terry Mathieu on OurValues.org, March 15, 2011.

In his opening statement, re-published on his official web site, King stated, "Let me make it clear today that I remain convinced that these hearings must go forward. And they will. To back down would be a craven surrender to political correctness and an abdication of what I believe to be the main responsibility of this committee—to protect America from a terrorist attack. Despite what passes for conventional wisdom in certain circles, there is nothing radical or un-American in holding these hearings."

> *"I believe Rep. King's hearings are vitally important, as too many Americans seem to be burying their heads in the sand. The 'millions of peace-loving Muslims' are not the problem."*
>
> **Posted by Terry Mathieu on OurValues.org, March 15, 2011.**

Many Democrats opposed the hearings and signed a letter sent to King to voice their concerns. The letter was co-sponsored by U.S. Rep. John Dingell, whose Michigan district is home to one of the largest Arab-American populations in the United States. The letter said, in part: "We are … deeply concerned that the stated narrow scope and underlying premises of these hearings unfairly stigmatizes and alienates Muslim-Americans. We ask that you reconsider the scope of these hearings and instead examine all forms of violence motivated by extremist beliefs, rather than unfairly focusing on just one religious group. We believe that the tone and focus of these hearings runs contrary to our nation's values." The National Jewish Democratic Council issued a statement that said, in part, that the hearings would be "detrimental because they target and single out one community, solely based on its religious affiliation. American Jews— and all Americans concerned about the rights of religious minorities, upon which this country was founded—should be deeply troubled about the chilling effect calling out Muslims through a congressional hearing can and will have on religious tolerance."

"McCarthy didn't have any evidence and many Americans lives were ruined. King, like McCarthy, will be basing his claims off of patriotism and nationalism. Attaching those themes to any idea often dismisses the need for evidence."

Posted by Persepolislost on OurValues.org, March 16, 2011.

Many Americans are struggling to draw conclusions from these contentious hearings and the larger issues they represent. An obvious conclusion is that these issues are here to stay for the foreseeable future. One reason is that these hearings had popular support. A majority of Americans (56 percent) felt that the King hearings on Muslim radicalization were a good idea, according to a poll taken by the Public Religion Research Institute in 2011 before the actual hearings. That's about the same level of support reported in a USA Today/Gallup poll around the same time. Less than a third of Americans (29 percent) thought the King hearings were a bad idea.

"Peter King missed an opportunity to investigate some serious threats to the safety of Americans. Instead he chose to demagogue an issue and benefit himself. He is helping to divert Americans away from some real and growing threats that may become even more dangerous and thus is doing a great disservice to America. It is pernicious. It is a shame."

Posted by Bob Bruttell on OurValues.org, March 16, 2011.

A dose of history might improve the debate. "It's easy to forget," writes columnist Bill Tammeus in his blog Faith Matters, "that some of the roots of terrorism were fertilized by official and unofficial American policy and action." No one has a monopoly on homegrown terrorism. Since 9/11, we've seen terrorism by white supremacists, anti-government/tax extremists, Christian extremists and Jewish extremists. Domestic terror organizations cover the map, and have included the Animal Liberation Front, Army of God, Aryan Nations, Ku Klux Klan, Jewish Defense League, Alpha 66 (Cuban exiles) and many more. But the possibility of homegrown Muslim terrorism seems to arouse a special anxiety in the hearts of many Americans.

> *"According to the Southern Poverty Law Center, hasn't the biggest rise in hate groups and expressions that could lead to violence been directed at President Obama by white nationalists and supremacists? These people pose a huge amount of work for the Secret Service."*
>
> **Posted by Bob Bruttell on OurValues.org, March 16, 2011.**

- Did you follow King's hearings? What did you think?

- What's your opinion of the threat of Muslim radicalization?

- Have you ever been singled out because of your race, gender or identity?

What do Muslim Americans Think About Islamic Extremism?

Are you concerned about the possible rise of Islamic extremism in America? If so, you are not alone. Two-thirds of all Americans report that they are very or somewhat concerned about this possible trend, according to a 2011 poll by the Pew Research Center. Seventy-two percent are worried about the rise of Islamic extremism around the globe.

Muslim-Americans express similar concerns. Sixty percent are concerned about the possible rise of Islamic extremism in America, and 73 percent are concerned about the rise of Islamic extremism elsewhere in the world.

Muslim-Americans see little support for extremism in their communities, according to the Pew survey. Only 6 percent say there is a great deal of support, with an additional 15 percent saying there is a fair amount of support. The general public has a different view. Fifteen percent say there is a great deal of support for extremism in Muslim-American communities. One in four (25 percent) say there is a fair amount of support. The general public is much more likely than Muslim-Americans to say that support for extremism in Muslim-American communities is increasing.

"The peace-loving Muslims need to stand up and repudiate the radicals."

Posted by Terry Mathieu on OurValues.org, March 15, 2011.

Muslim-Americans overwhelmingly reject suicide bombing as a legitimate way to defend Islam from its enemies. More than eight in ten say suicide bombing is never justified. Muslim-Americans also have a negative view of al-Qaeda. Seven of ten have very unfavorable views, and this number has been increasing over time.

"It is estimated that there are some 1.2 billion Muslims in the world, and that "only" 10 to 15 percent are of the radical variety. That still means that there are 120 to 180 MILLION radical Muslims in the world."

Posted by Terry Mathieu on OurValues.org, March 15, 2011.

Muslim-Americans believe that the majority of Muslim immigrants want to adopt American values and customs (though only a third of the general public agrees). Overall, Muslim-Americans are satisfied with their lives in the United States and happy to be here.

- How concerned are you about the rise of Islamic extremism in the U.S.?

- Do you personally know a Muslim?

- Why is it easier to generalize about a group when you don't personally know someone from that group?

- If you are Muslim, what's been your experience in the 9/11 decade?

National Security and Immigration

Are immigrants good or bad for America? Four of ten Americans say that immigrants threaten traditional American values, according to a 2013 poll by the Public Religion Research Institute (PRRI). But a majority (54 percent) of Americans say that the influx of newcomers from other countries strengthens our nation. Do you think immigrants strengthen or threaten the American way of life?

"For the wide majority of cases, immigrant values don't hurt individual Americans. Immigrant customs or traditions do not take away from current U.S. customs and traditions. On the contrary, immigrants have values that we might be able to learn from. If we remain open to exchanging ideas with people from different backgrounds, I think we'd be better off."

Posted by Gayle on OurValues.org, May 7, 2012.

Whatever your opinion, most Americans agree that our current system of immigration needs reform. Almost two-thirds of Americans say the current system is completely broken (23 percent) or broken but still working in some areas (40 percent), according to PRRI. An additional 29 percent say the system isn't broken but has big problems. Taken together, this means that more than nine of ten Americans see the need for immigration reform.

"Do we ever consider that maybe there are other people out there who might do things better than we do, or understand something better than we can? Immigrants bring more than just cheap labor to the U.S. They bring fresh new ideas."

Posted by Gayle on OurValues.org, May 7, 2012.

- What values should guide immigration reform?

- Should national security outweigh other values?

- Or, should compassion and humanitarian values take priority?

PRRI asked about eight different values that could guide immigration reform. Of these eight, which are the most important to you?

- National security
- Keeping families together
- Human dignity
- Enforcing the rule of law
- Fairness to taxpayers
- Golden Rule
- America's immigrant heritage

- Biblical example of welcoming the stranger

If you're like most Americans, two values would top your list: national security and the importance of keeping families intact. Eighty-four percent of Americans agree that each of these values should guide immigration reform. A close third is protecting the dignity of every person (82 percent), following by enforcing the rule of law (77 percent) and ensuring fairness to those who pay taxes (77 percent).

Republicans give very high priority to national security, with more than nine of ten saying that national security is an important value to guide reform. About eight of ten Democrats feel the same way.

"American values are what they are today because they are made up of all sorts of different values from all sorts of different places. So why should we stop integrating or accepting new values now?"

Posted by Gayle on OurValues.org, May 7, 2012.

How about the Golden Rule? In the survey, this was defined as "providing immigrants with the same opportunity I would want if my family was immigrating to the U.S." Almost seven of ten said this was an important principle. America's heritage as a nation of immigrants was also important, but fewer cited this value (52 percent).

About half of Americans cited the Bible's example of welcoming the stranger as an important or very important principle, putting this principle last on the list. Yet it is instructive that 50 percent of Americans do cite this value as an important one for guiding immigration reform. There's also a book, *Welcoming the Stranger*, by World Relief staffers that puts forth the Christian case for compassion in immigration reform.

- Do immigrants threaten or strengthen the American way of life?

- Should immigrants assimilate and adopt American values?

- Should national security be the most important principle guiding immigration reform?

Summarizing Security

National security is one of the Ten Core American Values. The events of 9/11 brought this issue to the forefront of our personal concerns and also our policies and priorities as a nation. New agencies were created to strengthen homeland security. The U.S. continues to spend enormous sums on the military in attempts to keep America safe and secure. A lot has changed in America since 9/11, but do you feel more secure?

National security often competes with other Core American Values such as freedom and respect for others. Opinions vary concerning the willingness to give up personal freedoms in return for stronger national security. This issue continues to be a challenge as we work out what it means to be both free and secure in America.

Since 9/11, our concerns about terrorism have focused on Muslims and Arabs in America, though homegrown terrorism is a bigger threat. We tend to focus our fears on specific groups, such as Arab-Americans and Muslims, in spite of data that challenges our perceptions. However, many Americans say that immigrants strengthen America. National security and enforcing the rule of law are important principles to guide immigration reform. But many Americans also believe that keeping families together and human dignity are important principles to keep in mind.

Perhaps, like Linus, we each have our own "security blanket." No matter what it is that provides a sense of national security for you, as a nation we remain focused and committed to this Core American Value.

Online resources to explore the topic of security are available at UnitedAmericaBook.com and include materials for group activities and online reader discussions.

CHAPTER 5

Self-reliance and Individualism

"I DID IT my way," sang Frank Sinatra in his classic 1969 release. Paul Anka wrote the lyrics to *My Way*. Many artists have covered this popular tune about self-reliance and individualism—doing things our own way.

"Self-Reliance" is the classic statement of American individualism. Ralph Waldo Emerson captured its essence in his 1841 essay by that title. "Trust thyself: every heart vibrates to that iron string," advised the Sage of Concord. Think for yourself. Don't conform. Follow your own path. Make your own way. Rely on yourself.

Does Emerson's message resonate with you? It does with most Americans. Self-reliance is one of the Core American Values. In this chapter, we'll look at different facets of self-reliance: what it means and how its meaning has evolved, the popular myth of the self-made man (or woman), how individualism informs our sense of right and wrong, the need to balance self-reliance with community and the paradoxical relationship of self-reliance and security. As you read this chapter, consider what self-reliance means to you and how this principle plays out in your life experiences.

> *"For what is a man, what has he got? If not himself,*
> *then he has naught. To say the things he truly feels*
> *and not the words of one who kneels. The record*
> *shows I took the blows and did it my way!"*
>
> **Lyrics to "My Way" by Paul Anka.**

Defining Self-reliance and Individualism

Individualism defines each person as a unique, independent and self-reliant entity. It is a value that emerged in Western civilization and attained a strong form in America. Individualism is "the first language in which Americans tend to think about their lives," wrote Robert Bellah and colleagues in *Habits of the Heart*. And, this language puts "independence and self-reliance above all else."

One difficulty with individualism as a concept is that it has different meanings. We use it here to refer to a strong preference for self-reliance. This is the main definition of individualism used in cross-cultural studies of values. For some, however, individualism means personal liberty. As defined in Chapter 3, liberty means being left alone to do what one wants, without restraint or interference. Recall that the rattlesnake ("Don't tread on me") was a symbol of liberty in colonial America. But liberty is not a Core American Value.

How do we know that self-reliance is a core value? Consider that more than eight of ten Americans agree with each of these statements: "I would rather depend on myself than on others" and "I rely on myself most of the time." It is remarkable how strongly Americans feel about these statements. Americans with a high school education (or less) are just as likely to agree with these statements as those with a college or even a graduate degree. Vast differences in income don't matter. Americans from different regions of the country are just as likely to agree with these statements. And, differences in race or religion don't matter. The wisdom of "trust thyself" is something on which even liberals and conservatives agree.

"I'm one of the 85% who depends on oneself, even when it's not wise. I learned in mid-life that really bright people ask for help. It's still tough for me, but I do it more than I used to."

Posted by Al Bamsey on OurValues.org, February 3, 2011.

Thomas Jefferson enshrined the ideal of individual autonomy and self-reliance in the Declaration of Independence. Jefferson's self-reliance and independent thinking are evident in his politics and philosophy, but also in his personal religious beliefs, his methods of farming and attitudes about the use of medicines. At the same time, however, he knew that self-reliance and responsibility go together.

"Ask not what your country can do for you—ask what you can do for your country."

John F. Kennedy

World surveys show that Americans are more individualistic than most other nationalities. American individualism is often contrasted with Asian collectivism. In an individualistic culture, "what is best for me" is a primary consideration when making decisions. Accomplishments and success are viewed in collective cultures as honoring family, ancestors, co-workers and community. In America, credit for success is typically attributed to an individual's hard work, talent and proficiency. In an individualistic, achievement-oriented society, those who win and those who lose get all the credit for the outcome. This orientation suggests that those who fail to get ahead suffer a defect of will, a lack of persistence, verve or some other personal shortcoming.

- Would you describe yourself as self-reliant?

- Would you rather depend on yourself than on others?

- Do you rely on yourself most of the time?

- When have you found yourself more dependent on others and less self-reliant?

- Have your ideas about self-reliance changed over the course of your life?

Self-reliance in the 1800s

The spirit of self-reliance goes back to colonial times and frontier days, but it gained prominence in the early 1800s. Members of the Transcendental Club, such as Emerson, criticized what they called the "pervasive materialism" of American culture. They called for a return to intellectual thinking, hard work and self-reliance.

"Discontent is the want of self-reliance; it is infirmity of will."

Ralph Waldo Emerson

"Self-control," "self-respect," "self-command" and "self-trust" were all phrases originally used by Emerson to express self-reliance. These additional phrases give us insight into his writing. His essays gave voice to the masses yearning to proclaim their independence and shape their own destinies. "Self-Reliance" helped define the role of individualism for a young nation facing numerous challenges, including war with Mexico, economic panic, the cruel displacement of Native American tribes, slavery and equal rights for women.

> "If an American is to amount to anything he must rely upon himself, and not upon the State; he must take pride in his own work, instead of sitting idle to envy the luck of others. He must face life with resolute courage, win victory if he can, and accept defeat if he must, without seeking to place on his fellow man a responsibility which is not theirs."
>
> **Theodore Roosevelt**

Emerson declared self-reliance and individualism as American virtues to a world that frowned on these very qualities. Self-reliance and personal individualism laid the foundation for remarkable accomplishment. The ensuing decade was a period of great American inventions, exploration, literary creativity and women's rights.

> "Chance never helps those who do not help themselves."
>
> **Sophocles**

Emerson's message affirmed that individual lives have inherent worth. Personal convictions and ideas are important. His colleague in the Transcendental Movement, Henry David Thoreau, put it this way in *Civil Disobedience*:

"The progress from an absolute to a limited monarchy, from a limited monarchy to a democracy, is a progress toward a true respect for the individual ... Is a democracy, such as we know it, the last improvement possible in government? Is it not possible to take a step further towards recognizing and organizing the rights of man? There will never be a really free and enlightened State, until the State comes to recognize the individual as a higher and independent power, and treats him accordingly."

- How do you define self-reliance? What phrases, words or images come to mind?

- When is self-reliance strength?

- When is self-reliance foolish?

Rags-to-Riches Myths

Generations of Americans have been motivated and inspired by Emerson's reassurance that their singular lives matter. Americans hold that personal convictions and individual talents can be cultivated to make America great. The rugged individualist represents this stereotype of American character: the loner who succeeds or fails based only on the person's abilities, effort and moral fiber. The Horatio Alger stories are one variation on this theme.

"It's hard to consider this a core value because of its deep mythical character. Is there data suggesting that Horatio Alger stories were the norm even when first written?"

Posted by John Hawthorne on OurValues.org, February 4, 2011.

The image of the self-made man or woman is a strong myth in America, captured during the Gilded Age in the stories of Horatio Alger. Alger rose from humble origins himself and graduated with honors from Harvard in 1852. Before his death in 1899, he wrote more than 100 books depicting young men who, through pluck, luck, hard work and sturdy moral principles rose from rags to riches.

"God helps those who help themselves."

From ancient Greece, also used by Benjamin Franklin.

Horatio Alger created his all-time, best-selling character in Ragged Dick, a hard-luck boy from the big city streets who learned vital lessons about core values. The original stories were serialized in *Student and Schoolmate,* a periodical especially aimed at children still in school. Ragged Dick's rise from utter poverty to success and fame was so hugely popular that the character became the model for other characters in several novels by Alger. Ragged Dick starred in six Alger novels. Today, one finds 21st century versions of Horatio Alger in the thousands of self-help books that offer the tips and tricks of success.

"There is always the "tinkering in the garage" story where someone makes good, but that is offset by the large percentage of entrepreneurial failures that run alongside the successes."

Posted by John Hawthorne on OurValues.org, February 4, 2011.

It's interesting to note that Ragged Dick never attained what today would be considered the financial status of the wealthy. Rather, he achieved middle-class security and respectability. Alger hoped to instill in America's youth the idea that self-reliance, strong moral character and luck would lead to success. It gave hope to many young Americans at a time of great social and economic upheaval in America.

"I have mentioned Dick's faults and defects, because I want it understood, to begin with, that I don't consider him a model boy. But there were some good points about him nevertheless ... He would not steal, or cheat, or impose upon younger boys, but was frank and straightforward, manly and self-reliant."

Excerpt from Alger's' 1868 novel, Ragged Dick: Street Life in New York with the Boot-Blacks.

Of course, the myth of the self-made man or woman is just that—a myth. Many forces larger than the individual affect our fates. It is somewhat ironic, for example, that today there are Horatio Alger scholarships! If success were all about hard work and moral determination, why would anyone need the support of a scholarship institution?

"This is clearly tied up in rugged individualism. If I'm special, there's nothing to hold me back. Anything is possible!"

Posted by John Hawthorne on OurValues.org, February 4, 2011.

- What "self-help" books have you found to be helpful?

- Have "self-help" books ever hindered your life?

- Do you relate to the "Rags to Riches" stories?

- Success for Alger was middle-class respectability. What are your markers of success?

Self-reliance: Who Decides Right and Wrong?

Self-reliance is almost universally held as a core value. If Americans say they rely on themselves most of the time and they prefer it that way, then who decides what's right and what's wrong? Since almost all Americans believe in self-reliance, we might expect most to agree that it's up to each person to decide. "Trust thyself. Decide for yourself." But that's not true. Only a third of Americans agree that what is right and wrong is up to each person to decide, according to my surveys.

"Each person deciding what's right is also called anarchy. That's why presumably we elect representatives to decide right and wrong."

Posted on OurValues.org by unattributed.

If it's not up to the individual, on what should right and wrong be based? A majority of Americans say "God's law," according to my national surveys. Emerson also understood the limits of self-reliance. He proclaimed in numerous sermons that the "origin of self is God." This theology shaped his writings, his actions and his life.

But unlike the belief in self-reliance, belief in "God's law" as the source of moral truth is not as universally held. Older Americans, for example, are much more likely than younger Americans to agree that right and wrong should be based on "God's law."

In fact, we see multiple divisions in beliefs about "God's law" as the basis of right and wrong. Southerners, political conservatives and conservative Christians strongly agree that this is the basis of right and wrong. Westerners, political liberals, and mainline Christians (along with members of other religions and the unaffiliated) tend to disagree.

"Judeo-Christian values guided our Founding Fathers and have served us well for over 200 years. We have built the strongest, most prosperous nation on earth. If it ain't broke, don't fix it!"

Posted on OurValues.org by unattributed.

Americans have always been unusual in the degree to which we hold the individual to be the judge of what's right and wrong. Critics of American character blame the supremacy of the individual as the cause of everything from divorce and abandonment of children to violence and disregard of one's fellows. But reality is more complex. The individualistic impulse is not expressed by going it alone, but by voluntarily joining groups and forming relationships, as paradoxical as this might seem.

"The greatest evil perpetrated on mankind has been committed by men who were certain they were right."

Posted on OurValues.org by unattributed.

Choosing where to live, to work, to worship and who to marry or befriend is the way Americans meet their social needs. Growing security, affluence, and the proliferation of voluntary groups of all kinds have given Americans more ways to join and belong—and more ways to exit as they see fit, as sociologist Claude S. Fischer concludes in *Made in America: A Social History of American Culture and Character.*

We haven't been corrupted by a rising focus on the self. "Americans did not turn into free lovers, free thinkers, ramblers, rebels or anarchists," says Fischer. "They remained by

Western standards remarkably committed to family, church, community, job and nation." The freedom to sever social bonds is matched by the requirement of commitment to those groups one elects to join.

- How do you decide what is right and what is wrong?

- Who or what influences your moral compass?

- Do you believe that deciding what's right or wrong should be based on God's law?

- If yes, then who do you trust to interpret God's law?

Balancing Self-reliance and Community

Americans, indeed, have a broad consensus around core values. Yet, there is also a widespread feeling of unease in the country. In *Our Divided Political Heart: The Battle for the American Idea in an Age of Discontent*, E.J. Dionne describes the polarization narrative that prevails in politics today. The result is our inability to have constructive debate, agree on facts or find common ground. Perhaps the recognition that Americans have never lost their core values could be a starting point for common ground and constructive debate.

For the better part of the last century, there was what Dionne calls "the Long Consensus" based on a balance of "our love of individualism and our reverence for community." But, he says, this consensus has fallen apart. Rebuilding it will require admitting that we can't boil things down to a single American trait like radical individualism. Our strength as a nation comes from the balance of individualism and community.

What does "too much" individualism mean? Here is an interesting example from the U.S. Army. "Be All You Can Be" was the Army's slogan for decades. In 2001, "Army of One"—a slogan that tapped into core American values of self-reliance and individualism, replaced it. Effective advertising always taps values. However, because this slogan downplayed teamwork and mutual support—essential and indispensable aspects of an effective military—it was short-lived. "One" actually was an acronym for "Officers, NCOs and Enlisted" but this was not well-communicated. Around Veterans Day 2006, "Army Strong" replaced "Army of One." "Army of One" promoted the American ideal of self-reliance but lacked a key ingredient for success—teamwork and mutual support. It didn't work.

Perhaps the character of America is best expressed in the balance of our core values. Without the equilibrium provided by other values—like respect for others, justice and fairness—self-reliance and rugged individualism become selfish and dysfunctional. Fortunately, contrasting values provide a balance in American life.

- When have you felt the tension between individualism and community?

- Where do you find common ground on this issue?

- Do you think it's possible to rebuild the "Long Consensus" of community and individualism? Why or why not?

Self-reliance and Security

How does the core value of self-reliance relate to other core values, such as security? One way to look at this is gun ownership. The gun is a symbol of self-reliance. Does owning a gun provide security?

My grandfather and great-grandfather owned guns. They grew up and lived in the Appalachian backcountry, a region well-known for its strong emphasis on self-reliance and distrust of government. When my grandfather went to work in the coalmines, he packed security in his lunch pail: a loaded pistol. My great-grandfather killed three men in self-defense. Fearing frontier justice, he fled over the mountains and never returned to his birthplace. Later in life, he used his double-barreled shotgun to harass the tax collector who claimed he hadn't paid his taxes.

My grandfather and great-grandfather were self-reliant and owned guns, but were they more secure?

> *"The United States is unique in the fact that it's probably the most individualistic culture in the entire world—we strive to live independently and associate asking for help with weakness. But the reality of it is that we all have limitations, and hit points when we simply cannot do things without the help of others."*
>
> **Posted by Gayle C. on OurValues.org, February 3, 2011.**

Today, gun owners are more likely to name "protection" as the reason why they own guns. Almost half (48 percent) give this reason, according to a 2013 survey by the Pew Research Center. Hunting is the second most frequently cited reason, given by 32 percent of gun owners. Only 2 percent said the main reason was their Constitutional right or cited the Second Amendment (the right to keep and bear arms).

Most gun owners (79 percent) say that owning a weapon makes them feel safer. A majority of the general public (58 percent) worry that stricter gun control laws would make it more difficult for people to protect themselves, their homes and their families. Even among those who don't own guns, the gun remains a symbol of self-reliance.

Putting the gun issue aside, we do know that Americans have come to live in increasingly secure conditions. This isn't true for all people, of course. But a growing proportion of Americans no longer fear sudden death from violence, accident or rampant disease, notes Fischer in *Made in America*. Increasing numbers can count on getting enough to eat (though millions of Americans today live in food-insecure households). A social safety net keeps people out of abject poverty, especially the old and the young. Comfort rather than mere survival has become a daily experience.

Increasing security actually strengthened the principle of self-reliance. Security gave more Americans the confidence and ability to examine and improve themselves, to pursue life courses of their own choosing, and to join or leave groups at will. Today, we are self-reliant because we are secure.

- Do you own a gun? If so, does it make you feel safer?

- What level of security do you feel in your own life?

- Does security make you more self-reliant?

Summarizing Self-reliance

The image of the rugged, self-reliant individualist remains strong in American culture. Most Americans would rather depend on themselves than on others. The ideal of self-reliance takes form in myths like the Horatio Alger rags-to-riches stories. We want to believe there are no limits to what we can accomplish. If we work hard we can "pull ourselves up by our bootstraps" and succeed. We tend to downplay the effects of socio-economic status, gender, race, education and opportunity that may limit our ability to rise to the top. We hold on to the exceptional success story and ignore the statistics.

Some worry that radical individualism has become rampant. In a culture that, by world standards, is unusually self-reliant, independent and freethinking, Americans must seek the balance between depending on self and realizing our need for cooperation and community.

Originally, America, like the rest of the world, was an agrarian society. We cultivated the land, grew our own food, treated our own illnesses and even taught our own children. Industrialization, world wars and the modern era have resulted in our evolving perceptions of what it means to be self-reliant, yet individualism still reigns. The freedom to enter and exit groups and relationships is stronger than ever. Increasing security has actually enabled more people to be self-reliant.

Online resources to explore the topic of self-reliance and individualism are available at UnitedAmericaBook.com and include materials for group activities and online reader discussions.

CHAPTER 6

Equal Opportunity

THESE FIVE WORDS—
"ALL men are created
equal"—may be the most
famous and powerful words
in American history. Thomas
Jefferson wrote these immortal words in the Declaration of
Independence. The application
of this principle, however, was
restricted—it didn't apply to
slaves, women, Native Americans or many others.

These five words have
shaped the course of the
nation as various groups strug-
gled for equal rights. Elizabeth Cady Stanton included the
words "all men and women are created equal" in the Declaration of Sentiments presented at the 1848 Seneca Falls

Convention, the first women's rights convention in the United States. Abraham Lincoln repeated the original five words in the Gettysburg Address (1863), as did Martin Luther King, Jr. in his "I Have a Dream" speech (1963). Today, persons with disabilities struggle for access, returning veterans struggle for jobs, same-sex couples struggle for marriage equality and the list goes on ...

"I believe the declaration that 'all men are created equal' is the great fundamental principle upon which our free institutions rest."

Abraham Lincoln

Equal opportunity is a Core American Value. In this chapter, we will explore the many facets of equality: equal opportunity versus equal outcomes, Martin Luther King Jr. and his legacy, the complexities of race and identity, economic justice, marriage equality and the plight of many returning veterans. We conclude by asking: Is America still the land of opportunity? As you read this chapter, consider what equality means to you and how this core value plays out in your life.

Defining Equal Opportunity

There are many types of equality, but equal access to jobs, a shot at success, and voting are chief among them. More than 90 percent of Americans endorse the value of equal opportunity. Conservatives and liberals, for example, agree that everyone should have an equal shot at what life has to offer. This means fair competition for jobs, promotions and other opportunities—free from discrimination based on race, age, gender, or other factors. When women are paid less than men for doing the same jobs, or a person is denied a job just because he or she is over 50, we don't have equal opportunity.

Over the years, Americans have demanded more equality of opportunity, and the historical record shows that opportunities have expanded over time. However, this expansion has not included all groups, and the application of the principle of equal opportunity is still being tested and worked out in American life. We will take a closer look at these situations.

Equal Outcomes?

Does equal opportunity translate into equal outcomes? Americans agree about the value of equal opportunity, but the same can't be said about the value of equal outcomes. This type of equality focuses on the distribution of end results, such as wealth and income. Americans who support equal outcomes usually don't mean that income or wealth differences should disappear altogether. Rather, they support laws and policies that reduce economic inequality. The minimum wage is one example, which sets a minimum hourly wage that a worker can be paid. Progressive taxation, where the rich pay a higher tax rate than the poor, is another example.

"If by 'equality of outcomes' one means that two people with the same goals, intelligence, and work ethic should be able to attain the same level of success regardless of where they start in life, then I absolutely agree with equality of outcomes in that sense."

Posted by Roberto Valenzuela on OurValues.org, February 8, 2011.

While Americans rally around the idea that everyone should have equal opportunities, most do not feel as strongly about a guarantee of equal income or standard of living. Compared to citizens of other rich nations, Americans are less worried about economic inequality and less willing to support redistributive policies. In a 2011 Gallup survey, 70 percent of Americans said that it was extremely or very important for the federal government to increase equality of opportunities. But only 46 percent felt it was as important for the government to enact policies to reduce the gap between rich and poor.

"Schools, the institutions traditionally called upon to correct social inequality, are unsuited to the task; without economic opportunity to follow educational opportunity, the myth of equality can never become real. Far more than a hollow promise of future opportunity for their children, parents need jobs, income and services. And children whose backgrounds have stunted their sense of the future need to be taught by example that they are good for more than they dared dream."

Kenneth Keniston

Just how big is the gap between rich and poor? Consider these three choices, posed by Michael I. Norton and Dan Ariely in a national survey of American attitudes toward inequality:

Picture the distribution of wealth in three different countries:

1. A country that shows perfect equality—everyone is equally wealthy.
2. A country that shows moderate inequality—the richest one-fifth of the population control 36 percent of the nation's wealth, with the poorest one-fifth controlling 11 percent of the wealth.
3. A country that shows extreme inequality—the richest one-fifth controls 84 percent of the wealth, and the poorest one-fifth with 4 percent.

Now, suppose you could join any of these countries but you would be randomly assigned to one of the wealth groups. So, for example, in the third country you were just as likely to end up in the super-rich group (84 percent of the wealth) or the super-poor group (4 percent of the wealth). Obviously, your life would be quite a bit different if you landed in one compared to the other!

"This is yet another good example of that famous American cognitive dissonance. Not many like where we are or where we appear to be going, but all the alternative paths are socialistic, Marxist or otherwise simply un-American."

Posted by Jlm Todd on OurValues.org, September 27, 2010.

What's your choice? How do you think Americans responded?

The two economists who conducted the survey learned that almost all Americans (92 percent) chose No. 2—a preference for moderate inequality over extreme inequality. What this meant is that nine of ten Americans preferred Sweden to the United States. The choices numbered 2 and 3 above represent the distribution of wealth in Sweden and the United States respectively.

"Democracy extends the sphere of individual freedom, socialism restricts it. Democracy attaches all possible value to each man; socialism makes each man a mere agent, a mere number. Democracy and socialism have nothing in common but one word: equality. But notice the difference: while democracy seeks equality in liberty, socialism seeks equality in restraint and servitude."

Alexis de Tocqueville, Democracy in America **(1831)**

The Swedish distribution was preferred by just about everyone—men and women, rich and poor, Republicans and Democrats. Of course, this hypothetical choice is open to many interpretations. Yet it is an eye opener to see that so many Americans across the board chose a wealth distribution that is so much more equitable than what actually exists in America.

"There can be no equality or opportunity if men and women and children be not shielded in their lives from the consequences of great industrial and social processes which they cannot alter, control or singly cope with."

Woodrow Wilson

The wealth gap is so large right now that an outside observer might conclude that America is a developing nation. Economic inequality in the United States places the nation 41 out of 136 countries, according to the CIA World Factbook. This means that inequality is lower in 95 other nations around the world. Countries that are similar to the United States include Mozambique, Jamaica, Bulgaria, Uruguay, Philippines, Cameroon, Guyana and Iran. Sweden has the lowest inequality of all 136 nations.

Economic inequality in American is at an all-time high. This gap between rich and poor reached record levels in 2008 right before the crash. The ensuing global recession aggravated the divide. It is the widest it has been since 1929. Disparities in wealth are even greater now. More and more wealth is concentrated at the top and the poor are getting poorer. The middle class is ailing, occupying a fragile place between the rich and poor.

• Which wealth distribution did you choose?

• Were you surprised to learn that Choice 3 is the United States?

• Is the gap between rich and poor too wide, too narrow, or just about right?

Another example is the inequality between CEO pay and the typical worker's pay. This gap has grown in leaps and bounds. In 1965, CEOs of big American companies earned 24 times the typical worker's pay, according to the Economic Policy Institute, a non-partisan think tank. In 2007, the difference was 275 times the typical worker's pay. The average CEO's compensation had increased 167.3 percent from 1989 to 2007. In the same period, the compensation of the typical worker had risen by only 10 percent. Wages haven't gone up much, but productivity has gone up a lot.

Surprised?

"I don't think there will ever be equality of outcomes and we shouldn't try to aim for that ..."

Posted by Kim on OurValues.org, February 7, 2011.

The huge gap between CEO and worker pay in America has no rival around the world, according to the EPI's statistics. The United Kingdom is the only nation that comes close. Other than the U.K., all European nations and Japan have much smaller ratios of CEO to worker pay.

What are the social and political consequences of extreme inequality? In a congressional hearing a few years ago, Alan Greenspan, former Federal Reserve chairman, said that increasing income inequality "is not the type of thing which a democratic society, a capitalist democratic society, can really accept without addressing." Is rising income inequality incompatible with our capitalist democratic society, as Greenspan said? His use of two adjectives to describe our society points to an inherent tension: inequality is bad for democracy, but it is an outcome of capitalism.

> *"Mere equal treatment before the law is insufficient, since it does not truly provide everyone in a society an equal opportunity to pursue his or her dreams."*
>
> **Posted by Roberto Valenzuela on OurValues.org, February 8, 2011.**

Increasing inequality erodes community, our trust of one another, and the extent to which we help one another. Robert Putnam found, for example, that more inequality means lower social capital. The growing divide may be another long-lasting outcome of our economic times—and with it, the continuing erosion of our social fabric.

> *"Equal opportunity is helping disadvantaged individuals receive access to the same level of opportunity as the more privileged."*
>
> **Posted by Roberto Valenzuela on OurValues.org, February 8, 2011.**

- Are you concerned that pay inequality in America has risen disproportionately compared to other developed countries?

- Do you worry about the social and political consequences of the widening wealth and income gap?

- Do we have a moral obligation to help those who are less fortunate than ourselves?

> *"All the citizens of a state cannot be equally powerful, but they may be equally free."*
>
> **Voltaire**

Celebrating MLK Day: A Personal Story

Martin Luther King, Jr. was a champion of equal opportunities for all Americans. Each year we celebrate his dream on Martin Luther King Jr. Day, one of only four federal holidays honoring an individual. What does MLK Day mean to you? Here's what it means—as seen through the eyes of a young boy, my son.

On the morning his school was commemorating Dr. King and his legacy, my son insisted on dressing in his Sunday best, because, he told us solemnly, there was an "important assembly." After school, I asked him about it. He said the entire school assembled, and he and his fellow second graders sang, "I've been to the mountaintop." He recited it for us, indicating that a considerable investment of time and energy had gone into learning the piece. Other grades gave their own performances honoring Dr. King.

What did the assembly mean to him? I knew that he was excited about a holiday from school, but I wondered what he took to be the meaning of the day. Here's what he said: "It means that the spirit of Martin Luther King's dream is still around."

What's his dream? I asked. "He wanted black people to have the right rights," he said. "Not to be slaves or bossed around and have to go to different schools and drink from different water fountains. He wanted blacks and whites to go to the same schools. He wanted justice for all—for everyone to have peace and to stop fighting."

- When did you have a personal experience that helped you realize the importance of equal opportunity?

- Describe an MLK Day celebration or event that was particularly meaningful for you.

- Is it important to you that schools, churches and other organizations honor MLK Day? Why or why not?

The Struggle for Equal Opportunity:
Letter From a Birmingham Jail

Martin Luther King Jr., champion of civil rights, was thinking of his own children as he penned his now-famous letter from a jail cell in Birmingham, Alabama, in 1963. His dream meant that parents like King would no longer have to explain to their children why certain places were off limits to people of color.

"All of us do not have equal talent, but all of us should have an equal opportunity to develop our talents."

John Fitzgerald Kennedy

King had been confined after arrest for his role in the Birmingham Campaign, a strategy of nonviolent direct action in protest of discrimination. Known now as the "Letter from Birmingham Jail," it was King's lengthy response to "A Call for Unity," a letter written by eight white clergy in the area and published in a local newspaper. They acknowledged social injustices, but called for an end to the demonstrations and acts of civil disobedience, arguing that the courts and negotiation should be used instead. In his letter, King argued that unjust laws would never fall without direct action.

A crucial part of King's letter reads: "We have waited for more than 340 years for our constitutional and God-given rights. The nations of Asia and Africa are moving with jet-like speed toward gaining political independence, but we still creep at horse-and-buggy pace toward gaining a cup of coffee at a lunch counter."

King goes on to give a list of reasons why justice could no longer wait. He includes experiences he had with his children. I am a father of a young child; you read my son's words above. I was struck by King's words: "We can no longer wait," King said, "when you suddenly find your tongue twisted and your speech stammering as you seek to explain to your 6-year-old daughter why she can't go to the public amusement park that has just been advertised on television, and see tears welling up in her eyes when she is told that 'Funtown' is closed to colored children, and see ominous clouds of inferiority beginning to form in her little mental sky, and see her beginning to distort her personality by developing an unconscious bitterness toward white people; when you have to concoct an answer for a 5-year-old son who is asking: 'Daddy, why do white people treat colored people so mean?'"

What's our answer to King's question today? A dream is something that is never fully realized—it's an ideal—but we have made progress in realizing King's dream of equality for people regardless of color. There is still a long way to go.

> *"I want to state upfront, unequivocally and without doubt: I do not believe that any racial, ethnic or gender group has an advantage in sound judging. I do believe that every person has an equal opportunity to be a good and wise judge, regardless of their background or life experiences."*
>
> **Sonia Sotomayor**

Everyone wants their children to have a seat at the table, but no one "owns" the table. The trend, the big historic shift since King's time, is that we are becoming a society of minorities. That's true in some regions of the United States more than others. The shift is far from complete. King's dream is imperfectly realized. But there is movement.

- Have you ever experienced unjust treatment because of race, gender or religious beliefs?

- Have you witnessed unjust treatment of others?

- Where do you see room for improvement in the treatment of minorities?

- How do you feel about the statement: "We are becoming a society of minorities"?

More Questions From Our Children

My son has contemplated the complexities of race and identity in America. The second question he asked me was this: "Daddy, is it okay to be white?" That stopped me in my tracks. I didn't know what to say. So, I took refuge in the strategy parents have used since the beginning of time: I stalled. He didn't persist, but I felt an important moment was in front of us. I had to say something. But what should I say?

Let me give you some background. We moved to our current neighborhood when he was only a year old. A chief reason we chose the area was to be in walking distance of a public elementary school known for high-quality academics and diversity. The student body is racially and ethnically diverse. About half are white and half are people of color. More than 20 languages are spoken at home among the families. My son says that one of the best things about the school is, in his words, "You can be friends with different people."

This blend of American and world cultures provides unparalleled opportunities for education in diversity, ethics and values. Martin Luther King Jr. Day ranks high in the many events celebrated at the school and used as occasions for moral education. The school hosts an annual International Night when children and families dress and give performances that highlight their cultural heritages.

Dr. King's children asked him, "Daddy, why do white people treat colored people so mean?" Half a century later, my son asked me, "Daddy, is it okay to be white?"

"I hope that people will finally come to realize that there is only one 'race'—the human race—and that we are all members of it."

Margaret Atwood

He and I have watched and discussed Dr. King's "I Have a Dream" speech. We watched President Obama's first inauguration together. We don't let him watch the news, but when he heard at school about floods in the Midwest and was frightened, we watched some media coverage. In it, a commentator mentioned that a "white house" was partially submerged and showed a picture of a white mansion with waters swirling around it. My son burst into tears, thinking that it was the White House in Washington, D.C., and that the president and his family were in danger.

Now back to his question. I did give him an answer. I've learned through trial and error that the best responses to my son are simple, straightforward, and short, with no professorial ramblings or (at least to me) fascinating digressions. I needed an answer that was truthful and direct, something appropriate for his age and capabilities.

"Until justice is blind to color, until education is unaware of race, until opportunity is unconcerned with the color of men's skins, emancipation will be a proclamation but not a fact."

Lyndon B. Johnson

My first, impulsive response, (which I didn't say) was flip: "Sure, of course it's okay to be white!" Not only would that have been flip, it wouldn't have addressed his question. Here's what I did say: "In the old days, it was okay only to be white. Now it's okay to be any color." "Old days" is our code word for the time of my childhood and before. He stopped what he had been doing, paused, and looked up at me. He was thinking, and I was waiting. "Oh," he replied.

I had to find out more, so I asked, "What made you think of your question?" He continued to look at me, thinking, and then took refuge in the strategy that children have used since the beginning of time: "I dunno," he said. And that was that.

What do you think of my response? If you have an alternative, please share it! So far, the issue has not come up again, but I'm sure it will and I'll need all the help I can get. I am left pondering what it all means. Why did he ask the question? What in his experience led to it? What does it tell us about our changing society?

- How would you have answered my son's question?

- What "difficult" questions have challenged you?

- Have you ever felt uncomfortable due to your race, gender or religious beliefs?

Economic Justice

Civil rights and racial equality were King's first concerns, but over time he increasingly emphasized economic justice. The billions of dollars spent on the Vietnam War, he thought, had diverted attention and resources away from the plight of millions of Americans at home. King felt this especially affected people of color, who lived their lives in poverty. Combating entrenched systems of poverty became a major focus in the final years of King's life. He was killed in 1968 while visiting Memphis to help rally sanitation workers on strike after years of unfair treatment.

The flaws in our society, King said in speeches and in his writings, were not superficial but systemic. In *Testament of Hope*, published after his death, he said, "Radical reconstruction of society itself is the real issue to be faced." A step in that direction was the "Poor People's Campaign," which he and the Southern Christian Leadership Conference organized in 1967 and launched in 1968. The focus of the "Poor People's Campaign" was jobs, income and housing.

The assassination of King sapped the energy of the "Poor People's Campaign." There were some events held after his death, but the campaign largely stalled. In 2003, there was an effort in Chicago to resurrect it but it didn't amount to much.

"Never be afraid to stand with the minority when the minority is right, for the minority which is right will one day be the majority."

William Jennings Bryan

- Does equal opportunity include economic justice?

- Do you believe that recent wars have affected your economic wellbeing and standard of living?

- Do you agree with King that the poor suffer more than others when resources are diverted to war efforts?

Marriage Equality

Should legal marriage be defined solely as a union of one man and one woman? Or, should it also include the union of two people of the same biological sex? The Defense of Marriage Act (DOMA) that Bill Clinton signed into law in 1996 restricted the legal definition of marriage to opposite-sex couples. At this writing, nine states and some Native American tribes sanction same-sex marriage, while others recognize civil unions. Yet other states have constitutional bans on same-sex marriage. In early 2013, the U.S. Supreme Court started hearings on same-sex marriage.

"For centuries, the definition of marriage has been defined as the union between one man and one woman. I have not changed my mind. I understand that others are entitled to their beliefs but so, too, am I."

Posted by tdk on OurValues.org, March 25, 2013.

Many advocates of same-sex marriage cite "equality" as the reason why they support it. The term "marriage equality" represents the argument that same-sex marriage is an application of the American principle of equality. Advocates also cite the principle of 'freedom,' arguing that legalized same-sex marriage is an application of this cherished value as well. (See Chapter 3 for more on the core value of freedom.)

> *"I have not changed my mind about same-sex marriage. I have always supported it because I believe my partner of 15 years and I have the same rights to life, liberty and the pursuit of happiness that heterosexuals do. It is appalling to be treated as a second-class citizen and I hope this will soon be a thing of the past."*
>
> **Posted by Amanda Udis-Kessler on OurValues.org, March 25, 2013.**

What do most Americans think? Many have changed their minds about gay marriage over the past decade and now support it, according to a 2013 study by The Pew Research Center. It is a dramatic shift in public opinion. As the authors of the report put it, "The rise in support for same-sex marriage over the past decade is among the largest changes in opinion on any policy issue over this time period. Fourteen percent of all Americans—and 28 percent of gay marriage supporters—say they have changed their minds on the issue in favor of gay marriage."

Why did people change their minds? Pew researchers asked the 14 percent to give their reasons. The main reason had little to do with values. Over a third (37 percent) said they changed their minds in favor of same-sex marriages because they have gay friends, family members or acquaintances.

The second most frequently cited reason, given by 25 percent, was increased tolerance, getting older, studying more or becoming more aware of the issue. Another 18 percent said they changed their minds because the world has changed, it's inevitable or it doesn't hurt anyone.

> *"It doesn't surprise me that the main reason people start supporting gay marriage is knowing someone who is LGBT. That way, the issue is not so easily written off. When it's someone you love you have to realize that they are people just like you. It's no longer "those people." It's "my son," "my daughter," etc. I am a proud supporter of marriage equality."*
>
> **Posted by bhile on OurValues.org, March 25, 2013.**

Freedom to choose was cited by fewer than two of ten Americans (18 percent). The figure is probably lower, because Pew put "love and happiness" in this category, too. And, only 8 percent gave equal rights as the reason why they changed their minds in favor of same-sex marriage.

- What's your position on same-sex marriage?

- How does the value of equal opportunity influence your views on same-sex marriage?

- If you are among the 14 percent who changed their minds in favor of gay marriage, why did you change your mind?

- Are you surprised to learn that knowing someone who is gay is a common reason why people changed their minds about same-sex marriage?

Equal Opportunity for Veterans: A New Minority?

Our military veterans are a new "minority" in our country, who now face many difficulties, such as high rates of homelessness, unemployment, post-traumatic stress, substance abuse, lack of formal education and marital problems. We've been at war for more than ten years, first in Afghanistan and then Iraq, and we have a lot of veterans who are struggling. More than four in ten (44 percent) say their re-entry and adjustment to civilian life has been difficult, according to a 2011 report by the Pew Research Center. Almost half of the veterans who saw combat say they suffer from post-traumatic stress.

"Our Nation must provide sufficient access to healthcare, adequate benefits and the supplemental resources our veterans were promised and so dearly need. We owe our heroes no less."

Dan Lipinski

A study by the Department of Housing and Urban Development and the Department of Veterans Affairs revealed a growing number of young veterans on the street as the Iraq and Afghanistan wars wound down. A disproportionately large number of the nation's homeless are veterans.

"As our brave men and women continue to return from the battlefields of the War on Terror, Congress must respond by enacting policies that meet the evolving needs of the veterans' community."

Randy Neugebauer

Pew researchers found that re-entry is easiest for commissioned officers and college graduates. Soldiers who were not officers or who didn't have a college education had a more difficult time. In addition, an experience that was emotionally traumatic decreases the odds of an easy re-entry, as does combat experience or knowing someone who was killed.

Married veterans who served in the last ten years find re-entry much more difficult than did married veterans from previous wars. This is a puzzling finding, but it goes to show that there's something unique about today's returning veterans.

Religion helps. Successful re-entry is much easier for veterans who frequently attend religious services, compared to those who do not.

> *"Caring for veterans shouldn't be a partisan issue. It should an American one."*
>
> **Jennifer Granholm**

Thousands of troops are returning home from the war in Afghanistan. This should be particularly concerning for all Americans as we consider economic justice, equal opportunity, and the future for those who served the country through military service.

How do Americans feel about our military veterans? Most Americans express pride in our troops. Three of four Americans say they have thanked members of the military for their service, according to the Pew report. Like many Americans, I have personally thanked soldiers for their service to our country, most often when I encounter them in an airport.

Other than that, however, the connection between the military and regular citizens isn't that close. "A smaller share of Americans currently serve in the armed forces than at any time since the peacetime era between World Wars I and II," say the Pew researchers. A tiny fraction of the populace— about 1/2 percent to 1 percent—has served on active military duty in the past ten years.

Most people don't understand that veterans face unique problems. What has happened, Pew researchers conclude, is a military-civilian gap. In their report, they quote military historian Rick Atkinson, who says that the military "has become a separate tribe in the republic."

Now, more than 40 years after King's death, we've spent trillions on new wars. The wealth gap is wider than ever. And, millions of Americans, including many veterans, live in poverty. We find a way to fund our wars but find it difficult to provide jobs, medical care and service for veterans. The focus of Dr. King's "Poor People's Campaign" on jobs, income and housing seems quite relevant today.

- Have you or a family member served in recent wars?

- Do you know veterans of the wars in Afghanistan or Iraq?

- How aware are you of the challenges veterans face?

- What are our responsibilities to veterans following military service?

Is America Still the Land of Opportunity?

Is the American dream fading? Most Americans embrace equal opportunity for everyone as a Core American Value, but younger Americans see a picture that is different from the one their parents saw when they were young. Young adults are especially hard hit by the bad economy and dim employment prospects. For many college-age Millennials (ages 18-24), the American dream of a better life has not become a reality. Indeed, only four of ten (40 percent) say that the American Dream is still true today, according to the Public Religion Research Institute's 2012 Millennial Values Survey.

These young adults don't have much faith in the fairness of our economic system. More than seven of ten college-age Millennials (73 percent) feel that our current system favors the rich. More than six of ten (63 percent) agree that "one of the big problems in this country is that we don't give everyone an equal chance in life." Those who lean Democratic are more likely to share these beliefs than those who lean Republican.

"It is time for us as members of generation Y to assert ourselves and figure out ways to help ourselves ... If the baby-boomers do not give us opportunities we need to give ourselves opportunities."

Posted by B. Campbell on OurValues.org, September 25, 2011.

Is America still the land of opportunity?

Two economists at the Brookings Institution, Isabel V. Sawhill and Ron Haskins, tackled the "land of opportunity" question by looking at cross-cultural evidence. If America is still the land of opportunity, Americans should have more economic opportunities than people living in other countries. However, say Sawhill and Haskins, "some other advanced economies offer more opportunity than ours does."

Compared to the United States, a child raised in a lower-income family of origin in the United Kingdom or Nordic countries like Denmark and Sweden has a better chance of creating a higher-income family in adulthood. Americans born into a middle-class family have only a 50/50 chance of improving their lot over time. They are just as likely to move down the economic ladder. And, Americans born into a poor family tend to stay poor. Immigrants, however, do better in America than they would have done in their countries of origin.

"In the early '90s, I had an opportunity to be in a group meeting with the Ambassador from Sweden at the Embassy. She had been here for over 20 years. She talked to us about her form of government, Social Democracy, which provides healthcare, job training, education, etc. for all its citizens. I knew then that this is what I wanted our government to aspire to. The most telling point she made was when someone asked her what she told her countrymen about life in the U.S. Her reply: 'I tell them the U.S.A. is a very great place to live if you are young, healthy and wealthy. If you are old, sick or poor it is a terrible place to be.' That answer has stayed with me over the years."

Posted by Susan L. on OurValues.org, September 27, 2010.

Generally, the standard of living in each generation has risen over time. But that's no longer true. "Today, men in their 30s earn 12 percent less than the previous generation did at the same age," write Sawhill and Haskins. "Women have joined the labor force in a big way, and their earnings have increased …. But with so many families now having two earners, continued progress along this path will be difficult unless wages for both men and women rise more quickly."

Equal opportunity is a core value, but the gap between the ideal of equal opportunity and reality appears to be widening.

- How has America been the land of equal opportunity for you?

- Do you think America is still the land of opportunity for young people today?

Summarizing Equal Opportunity

Ask most Americans and they will agree that equal opportunity for all is a Core American Value. This value is enshrined in the Declaration of Independence, though its actual practice was limited and many groups were excluded. America has struggled throughout her history to embrace and apply this core value. Dr. King devoted his life to the pursuit of civil rights and racial equality and increasingly spoke out against economic inequality. Yet today, economic inequality is at an all-time high.

We've come a long way since the 1960s but the struggle for equal opportunity is still just that: a struggle. Today, for example, same-sex couples struggle for marriage equality. A new "minority" segment of our population—veterans of recent wars—face enormous challenges.

Part of the "American Dream" is to live a better life than our parents. But America's youth have been hard hit. College-age Millennials no longer see America as the land of opportunity. The challenge, if we truly cherish the value of equal opportunity, is to blaze a path to make this a reality for all. The

American dream is just a dream without the work, sacrifice and resolve to make it a reality.

Online resources to explore the topic of equal opportunity are available at UnitedAmericaBook.com and include materials for group activities and online reader discussions.

CHAPTER 7

Getting Ahead

"WINNING ISN'T EVERY-
THING, it's the only thing,"
said legendary football coach
Vince Lombardi. Most of us
want to win, to achieve—to
be successful. We want to be
the best, belong to the best
organization, and live in the
best country. We applaud our
Olympic gold medal win-
ners and class valedictorians.
We consult bestseller lists to
decide which books to buy
for our e-readers or music to
download from the iTunes
store. Getting ahead and being the best is, well, the best.

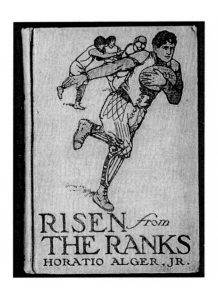

Getting ahead is a "moral mandate" in America, observed
sociologist Robert Merton. It is also a Core American Value.

Most Americans endorse getting ahead as a guiding principle and motivating force in their lives. Americans—regardless of age, race, religion, or other factors—place a premium on success. Getting ahead has been a part of our culture for a long time.

Getting ahead fits hand in glove with self-reliance (Chapter 5) and equal opportunity (Chapter 6). These values are mutually reinforcing. Equal opportunity describes a level playing field on which self-reliant individuals compete with one another and the best get ahead. We saw in Chapter 6 that the playing field isn't always level. This chapter will reveal that it isn't always the best or the smartest who get ahead.

In this chapter, we consider the multiple meanings of getting ahead, why second place is considered to be the first loser and the importance of monetary success. We explore the roles of intelligence, hard work and luck play in getting ahead. And, we evaluate America in five areas—health, equality, education, safety and democracy—to see if the nation is still #1.

Defining Getting Ahead

Getting ahead means "to be more successful, or to progress more quickly, than other people," according to the online MacMillan Dictionary. This definition is helpful because it points out that getting ahead is relative. Getting ahead is advancement relative to someone else. Of course, it's possible to have an internal measure of getting ahead, but usually advancement is judged in comparison to other people.

"If you're not the lead dog, the scenery never changes."

Robert Benchley (attributed)

The principle of getting ahead applies in countless areas of life. Monetary success and occupational advancement are indicators of getting ahead. But so are social mobility, successful relationships, weight lost and even spiritual development. There are many ways to get ahead.

- What does "getting ahead" mean to you?

- How do you define achievement and success?

- Do you feel you are getting ahead compared to the lives of your parents or your grandparents?

Is Second Place the First Loser?

Picture a medal ceremony at the Olympics. Three athletes stand on the podium—the three best in the world in their sport. Is each happy to be there? Study their facial expressions, and you'll see that they are not. One is especially unhappy. Is it the gold, silver or bronze medalist?

A team of psychologists studied the behavior and emotional reactions of Olympians and came to a clear conclusion: the silver medalist is the unhappiest athlete on the podium. The gold medalist is obviously thrilled to take the top spot. The silver medalist is thinking about "what might have been," say Victoria Medvec and colleagues in their study.

Thinking about what might have been is called "counterfactual thinking." For the silver medalist, "the most compelling counterfactual alternative … is winning the gold, whereas for the bronze medalist it is finishing without a medal." The silver medalist is filled with regret, ruminating about "what if …?" But the bronze medalist is happy—after all, the bronze medalist made it to the podium!

Silver medalists are sometimes called the first losers. Only one person (or team) wins a competition; everyone else is a loser.

> *"So we have the paradox of a man shamed to death because he is only the second pugilist or the second oarsman in the world. That he is able to beat the whole population of the globe minus one is nothing; he has 'pitted' himself to beat that one; and as long as he doesn't do that nothing else counts."*
>
> **William James (1892)**

The experience of the silver medalist illustrates the ambiguity of getting ahead in any area of life. Obviously, all three medal winners achieved a high degree of success, but only one athlete "won." What about all the athletes who didn't win any medals? They, too, achieved a mark of success just by making it to the Olympics. But they returned home empty handed. Getting ahead is ambiguous because it never ends—you'll never know when you get there, because "there" is a receding horizon.

- Did you ever come in second place? How did it feel?

- Do you consider silver medalists to be the first losers?

- How do you know when you have gotten ahead?

Monetary Success

Money is a means to an end (buying the goods and services we need and want). For many, money in and of itself is a goal. Money is a measure of success. Having money is a symbol of prestige and status. How much more money would it take for you to get ahead? The typical answer is about twenty-five percent more—no matter which income bracket a person is in. Of course, once income increases by twenty-five percent, we soon feel that it would take twenty-five percent more to get ahead.

> *"More. That's right, I want more."*
>
> **Johnny Rocco, played by Edward G. Robinson in the film**
> *Key Largo.*

Monetary success can be considered from many angles. Consider this one: can money buy happiness? Would more money improve the quality of your life, elevate your sense of wellbeing, and help you get ahead?

> *"Strive not to be a success, but rather to be of value."*
>
> **Albert Einstein**

There's good research on these questions, based on an analysis of Gallup survey data on wellbeing. Two psychologists, Nobel laureate Daniel Kahneman and Angus Deaton, considered 450,000 responses to Gallup's questions about emotional wellbeing and life evaluation. Emotional wellbeing refers to how a person felt a day before the survey (stressed, happy, angry, and so on). Life evaluation refers to the ladder scale: which rung your life is on today and which rung you expect to be on in five years.

Here's what they found out: Money buys a more positive evaluation of one's life. People steadily move up the ladder as their incomes improve. Even wealthy people experience this positive effect.

> *"I wouldn't say money buys happiness, but money will give you options, which will in turn make you happier."*
>
> **Posted by Emily T. on OurValues.org, October 25, 2011.**

Emotional wellbeing also improves as income rises. But other factors are more important in one's emotional life:

personal health, feelings of loneliness, smoking, caregiving and so forth. Consider that while emotional wellbeing rises with income, it hits a ceiling at an annual income of $75,000. After this figure, people don't report improvements in their daily emotional wellbeing. But could emotional wellbeing keep improving?

New research by economists Justin Wolfers, Daniel W. Sacks, and Betsey Stevenson shows that happiness increases as income increases—and there's no upper bound. As they put it, "there is no satiation point beyond which the relationship between income and wellbeing diminishes." In almost all countries around the world, more money means more happiness.

But there's a kicker for Americans. The size of the American economy, measured as GDP, has doubled in the last 40 years, but average wellbeing has declined. The economists point to a unique American trend as the culprit: rising economic inequality. Only a small fraction of the American people has experienced big increases in wealth and income. The super-rich must be much happier as a result, but they are so few in number that they don't affect average wellbeing. Most Americans have been left behind, casualties of the rising inequality trend.

"I will admit life is probably much easier when you have a higher income because you will likely have more opportunities. Now that I have a steady income, whereas I didn't for a short period of time, my life is less stressful because I don't have to worry as much about what I'll be able to buy at the grocery store or bills I need to pay. Money gives me the option to buy food, pay bills, etc. You could say money buys happiness in this sense, but it will never make someone completely happy."

Posted by Emily T. on OurValues.org, October 25, 2011.

- How much more income would it take to make you feel that you were getting ahead?

- How has money bought happiness for you?

- How has the amount of money you have influenced your emotional wellbeing?

Do the Smartest Get Ahead?

Why do some people get ahead and others don't?

Pour cream in your coffee and it rises to the top. Fancy coffee shops now create works of art based on that principle. But, when people repeat that line outside of cafés, they're usually talking about the dividing line between rich and poor. They're implying that it's only natural that the best rise to the top. The rich deserve to be rich. Those at the top deserve it because they're smarter, or better educated, or more talented, or work harder, or faster or have better ideas. What about those at the bottom? Well, they deserve their lot in life, too, because they lack all these great qualities.

The cream-to-the-top theory is often used to explain persistent inequality in America. As we saw in the previous chapter, the gap between rich and poor is at an all-time high. Do you buy the argument that the rich deserve their riches and the poor deserve their poverty?

"Success is to be measured not so much by the position that one has reached in life as by the obstacles which he has overcome."

Booker T. Washington

Wall Street is one place where the cream-to-the-top theory reigns supreme. Wall Street bankers consider themselves to be the "best and the brightest." They recruit the "best and the brightest" from elite schools, especially Ivy League schools like Harvard and Princeton. The select few get to work among and be what Tom Wolfe called "masters of the universe."

Anthropologist Karen Ho gives us a rare insider's view of Wall Street. She studied Wall Street bankers in their natural habitat, documenting their rituals, customs, language and culture in her book *Liquidated*. She was struck by how often people "ranked and distinguished themselves according to their 'smartness.' The term seemed fundamental to the Wall Street lexicon. My informants proclaimed that the smartest people in the world came to work there; Wall Street, in their view, had created probably the most elite-work society ever to be assembled on the globe."

"Success is a lousy teacher. It seduces smart people into thinking they can't lose."

Bill Gates

Ho describes what she calls a "culture of smartness" on Wall Street. This culture is a self-reinforcing system of beliefs, all wrapped around the idea that the "brightest people in the world" work on Wall Street. This culture gives Wall Street bankers the personal and institutional power "to enact their worldviews, export their practices and serve as models for far-reaching socioeconomic change." Since they are the smartest people on the planet, the rest of us should listen to and follow what they say.

> *"This American Life had a lengthy segment featuring interviews with Wall Street professionals who are angry with the Obama administration and the federal government in general for financial constraints placed on their profession ... Even though 'Wall Street' essentially crashed in a spectacular way ... and 'we' had to bail out the financial profession to keep it solvent, all the young professionals interviewed said their success depended on their own smarter-than-the-average-American business skills. It was pretty stunning to hear one after another argue strenuously that America is all about survival of the fittest—and that they deserve to survive and thrive because they're smarter than other people."*
>
> **Posted by David Crumm on OurValues.org, September 27, 2010.**

What is the role of raw intelligence? Some say that IQ or raw intellectual horsepower is the cream. However, a famous study looked into this, charting what happened to high-IQ individuals over the course of their lives. Some did very well in life, confirming the IQ theory. Others did pretty well. But a sizable proportion didn't do well at all. IQ, it turned out, was only one of many factors that explained outcomes in life.

> *"Americans can be competitive, and to be called a high achiever in the U.S. is quite a compliment."*
>
> **Posted on OurValues.org by unattributed.**

Malcolm Gladwell talks about this in his book *Outliers*. As a case in point, he describes the story of a man with an IQ of 195 (45 points higher than Einstein's) who, despite his gifts, ended up working on a horse farm in rural Missouri. What held him back, says Gladwell, was the environment in which he grew up. His environment was devoid of people who went to college (and would have known the ins and outs of the application process). He lacked the right type of cultural capital: an understanding of how the world really works, how to relate to authority and those in power, and knowledge of language and customs that are required to be successful.

"IQ alone is not enough. It is interesting to note that the rising inequality in America has more to do with the political choices that have been made than any simple explanation like education or IQ."

Posted on OurValues.org by unattributed.

- What do you think of the cream-rises-to-the-top theory? How have you seen this play out in your life and the lives of your acquaintances?

- What is your opinion of Wall Street? Do you consider them the "brightest and the best?"

- Do the smartest get ahead?

Does Hard Work Get You Ahead—or Luck?

Does hard work pay off? The Horatio Alger stories we talked about in Chapter 6 celebrate the idea that hard work pays off. But is getting ahead just plain luck?

A majority of Americans (55 percent) believe that hard work is the way to get rich, according to a 2013 poll by Rasmussen Reports. Only 10 percent say that getting rich is just luck. Over a third (36 percent) says that rich people simply inherited their money. Opinions about the formula for success differ dramatically by age. Americans under 40 are much less likely to say that hard work is the key to riches.

> *"Americans tend to view themselves as a 'class-less' society. Do we then underestimate the role of social status and connections in helping us get ahead? It is easy to negate barriers such as race, gender and religion in this process; especially if you are the right 'color,' gender and mainstream faith."*
>
> **Posted on OurValues.org by unattributed.**

The Rasmussen Reports poll also shows that six of ten Americans (59 percent) believe it's "no longer possible for anyone to work hard and get rich." Republicans and Democrats largely agree on this point. Almost half of all Americans (48 percent) believe it's still possible for people to work their way out of poverty—but the number of Americans who disagree has grown over time.

> *"Regarding poverty, my parents raised a very large family and worked their tails off. They never accepted food stamps or other government assistance ... although they most certainly qualified for it. In other words, I grew up dirt poor, but my parents taught me to work hard, obtain an education, maintain high moral standards, and to be grateful. I have found that gratitude is essential to happiness. I never knew I was poor until high school. And by then I had enough constitution of mind and character that it didn't matter."*
>
> **Posted by Jack on OurValues.org, December 14, 2011.**

A 2011 Reason-Rupe survey found even more support for hard work as the key to getting ahead. When asked to choose between "people get ahead by their own hard work" versus "lucky breaks or help from other people are more important," more than eight in ten (81 percent) chose hard work.

Only 15 percent chose lucky breaks or help from others. Tea Party members overwhelmingly chose hard work (89 percent). Republicans were a close second at 86 percent. Democrats were the least likely to choose hard work, but still three-quarters (74 percent) made this choice.

"Formula for success: rise early, work hard, strike oil."

J. Paul Getty

Some people might get ahead because of lucky breaks, but believing in luck can be harmful to your financial health and wellbeing. Economist Stephen Wu found that people who believe that luck influences their financial wellbeing recognize their need to save. However, these people are less likely to actually save money. People who feel they don't have much control over their lives are also less likely to save.

- Based on your personal experience, what is the formula for getting ahead in America?

- To what extent has hard work paid off for you?

- Have lucky breaks played a role in your success?

Does America Get an A+?

Most Americans, including me, think of our country as the best in the world. But are we still on top? Does America get an A+?

In *The Measure of a Nation*, Howard Steven Friedman answers this question. Friedman is a leading statistician and health economist for the United Nations. He compares the United States with other wealthy, large nations in five areas: health, equality, safety, education, and democracy.

Before we go on, I'll give you a warning: We don't fare very well in this comparison. And it's hard to argue with Friedman's facts. He uses high quality data to compare the United States with Australia, Belgium, Canada, France, Germany, Greece, Italy, Japan, Portugal, Netherlands, South Korea, Spain and the United Kingdom. The results of his comparison are grim.

Let's start with health. Here's how the U.S. ranks against these thirteen nations:

- Americans have the lowest life expectancy overall.
- American women have the lowest life expectancy.
- American men have the lowest life expectancy.
- America has the highest rate of infant mortality.
- America has the highest rate of maternal mortality (mother's death in childbirth or soon after).
- America has the lowest rate of return on health expenditures, meaning that we spend more than other nations and have the lowest life expectancy.

Shocking, isn't it? Unfortunately, America doesn't look much better in the other areas Friedman examined: equality, safety, education and democracy.

America is the leader in inequality, having the highest levels of both income and wealth inequality. The gap between rich and poor is growing faster in the U.S. than it is in other nations. The rich have gotten richer but the middle class has not. Wealth has not trickled down to wage earners, and incomes at the low end of the scale have grown at a much slower rate here than elsewhere in the world.

"I think the widening gap in income is a serious problem as of right now, but I don't think it will stay this way forever. I mean, those with the 'big' incomes need people with 'little' incomes to spend in order to keep receiving their 'big' incomes, right? Let's hope so."

Posted by Emily T. on OurValues.org, November 16, 2011.

How safe is it to live in America? The terror bombings at the 2013 Boston Marathon reminded us that enemies are internal as well as external. April 15, 2013, dawned as Patriots' Day, a holiday celebrated in Massachusetts and Maine. The weather was great and the Boston Marathon was well attended. Then, two crude bombs exploded near the finish line, placed and timed to inflict maximum damage. Three people were killed and many others seriously injured. The Boston area was locked down during the intensive manhunt in the days that followed, ending with the death of one suspect and the capture of the other.

The same week in April is the anniversary of past shootings and acts of homegrown terrorism, such as the Oklahoma City bombing, the killings at Columbine High School and the shootings at Virginia Tech.

If you look at the money we spend on police, prisons, and the military, it would seem that we should be safe and secure. Our budgets for safety and security are higher than those of other nations, but these investments don't seem to have paid off.

The rate of intentional homicides is much higher in the United States than it is in any comparable nation. In fact, it's more than double the rate of South Korea, which has the second highest rate. There is a downward trend in homicides in the United States, but we are still #1 among comparable nations.

Incarceration is one of our main responses to crime. America holds the top spot when it comes to the rate of incarceration. Not only do we throw proportionately more people in jail, sentences here are longer and harsher than elsewhere. Our military expenditures as a percentage of GDP are higher than other nations.

How peaceful are we as a nation, compared to others? The Global Peace Index can give us some insight. This index is composed of 23 indicators, such as number of conflicts fought, level of violent crime, access to weapons, incarcerated population, potential for terror attacks, access to weapons, disregard for human rights and so on. An index like this is fraught with difficulty and open to interpretation. Yet it is informative to know that the United States is rated the least peaceful nation of the set of nations compared in Friedman's book.

How about education? There's little doubt we have some of the finest universities in the world. The United States ranks #1 in average years of schooling for adults, compared to other large and rich nations. However, this top ranking actually reflects past investments in education. At one time, America was alone in providing mass public education, and specific investments like the G.I. Bill really paid off. But if we look at the expected years of school for kids who are starting their education, we see a different story—one that doesn't bode well for the future.

The United States ranks near the bottom in expected years of schooling. This means that an American child who enters school now is expected to end up with less education than the children of other nations.

Number of years in school is one thing; the quality of education during those years is another. The United States gets average to poor grades for quality of education: reading, math and science literacy. Looking at 15-year-old students, we're in the middle of the pack for reading literacy. For math and science literacy, we get poor grades. We're in the bottom third of the class of comparable nations, despite spending more money per student than any other nation.

How vital is our democracy? The comparisons with other nations reveal a gap between our perceptions and reality. America had the first modern design for democracy, but, as Friedman notes, we haven't fixed problems that have existed from the beginning. Perhaps the most glaring is the Electoral College system, which can allow one candidate to be elected president even though another candidate won the popular vote. This effect can be produced, due to the state-by-state winner-take-all policies of the Electoral College. That's not very democratic.

"We can have democracy in this country, or we can have great wealth concentrated in the hands of a few, but we can't have both."

Louis Brandeis

We have free elections, but the lowest voter turnout rate of any large, rich nation. Some nations have high turnouts because they have compulsory voting laws—Australia, for example. Most democracies don't, yet their voters still show up at the polls.

Our two-party system tends to stifle minority voices. America has never had a viable third party, but multi-party systems are the norm in democracies elsewhere. Multiple party systems often require building coalitions to run a country, leading to broader representation, inclusiveness and compromise. Our two-party system leads to political polarization.

- How do you feel about Friedman's critical evaluation?

- Of the five areas Friedman examined—health, equality, safety, education and democracy—which one is the most important to you?

- What would need to happen for America to improve and rise in rank in these five areas?

- What can America learn from other nations?

Summarizing Getting Ahead

Getting ahead is a moral mandate in America. It has driven generations of Americans to dream, strive and work toward success and all that success brings. Getting ahead is so important that we often think of second place as the first loser.

Monetary success is the indicator that usually comes to mind when we think of getting ahead. Money can't buy happiness, but it can improve life satisfaction and emotional wellbeing.

Many Americans subscribe to the theory that "the best and the brightest" rise to the top. Smarts and hard work are the keys to success. Lucky breaks matter, but they're not that important. The evidence shows that the story of success in America is more complicated. The smartest don't always rise to the top. Hard work pays off, but not for everyone.

Like individuals, nations also strive to get ahead—to be competitive in the world's society of nations. We like to think of America as #1, but America ranks near the bottom in comparisons with other affluent democracies. We aren't the leaders in health, equality, education, safety or even democracy.

Do Americans need to rethink "getting ahead" in terms of other qualities of life that contribute to meaning and wellbeing? Is the very notion of getting ahead in need of reform?

Online resources to explore the topic of getting ahead are available at UnitedAmericaBook.com and include materials for group activities and online reader discussions.

CHAPTER 8

Pursuit of Happiness

THE PURSUIT OF happiness is one of the fundamental rights named in the U.S. Declaration of Independence: "We hold these truths to be self-evident, that all men are created equal, that they are endowed by their Creator with certain unalienable Rights among which are Life, Liberty and the Pursuit of Happiness."

Since the time when Thomas Jefferson wrote these words, Americans have pursued happiness with a passion. The search for happiness is so strong that "hedonism" is a Core American Value. Hedonism refers to the pursuit of pleasure and self-gratification. It is the belief that pleasure is the highest good, and that pleasure is the proper goal of life.

In this chapter, we define happiness and consider whether America is the happiest place on earth. We examine some of the false paths to happiness that many of us trod—searching for happiness in the consumption of things. We ask if marketing and advertising are to blame, and whether religion in the form of the "Prosperity Gospel" might play a role. We end the chapter with what psychologists have learned about the paths to true happiness, and how various practices connect to Core American Values.

Defining Happiness

What are we seeking when we pursue happiness? How do we define it? We know if we are happy or not, but it helps to have a precise definition.

Here's how psychologist Sonja Lyubomirsky defines it in her book, *The How of Happiness*—"the experience of joy, contentment or positive wellbeing, combined with a sense that one's life is good, meaningful and worthwhile." That certainly seems like a worthwhile pursuit!

• What does happiness mean to you?

- Is the pursuit of happiness one of your chief aims in life?

How Happy Are Americans?

Is America the happiest place on earth? The World Values Surveys have asked people around the world to rate their happiness. The results show that Americans aren't as happy as we might have hoped. The U.S. ranks No. 16 among the ninety-seven nations surveyed. Denmark is the happiest place in the world; Zimbabwe, the unhappiest.

"I believe that every human mind feels pleasure in doing good to another."

Thomas Jefferson

University of Michigan political scientist Ronald Inglehart, chief architect of the World Values Surveys, and colleagues tracked happiness trends since 1946. They learned that democratization and increasing social tolerance are among the key contributors to rising happiness around the world. "The results clearly show that the happiest societies are those that allow people the freedom to choose how to live their lives," says Inglehart.

"Happiness lies in the joy of achievement and the thrill of creative effort."

Franklin D. Roosevelt

"Happiness is not a goal; it is a by-product."

Eleanor Roosevelt

Happiness has increased in the majority of countries and several have experienced rapidly increasing levels of happiness over the past 60 years. The trend in the United States, however, is no trend. Happiness is flat when you look over the past sixty years. But if you turn up the resolution, you can spot shorter patterns. From 1946 to 1980, the happiness trend was downward. From 1980 to 2006, the happiness trend was upward. And, in the last few years we know that this upward trend reversed for many Americans.

Another way to look at it is that Americans have experienced lots of ups and downs in their emotional wellbeing. Most other economically advanced democracies have not. In these nations, happiness trends are generally upward.

- Are you happy?

- What makes you happy?

- How has your happiness changed over your life?

'Shiny Objects' and Happiness

The emphasis on leisure and consumption in America is unmistakable. According to the United Nations, if everyone in the world consumed resources at the level of Americans, we would need 4.05 planets annually to meet their requirements!

Every day in America, consumer spending is reported on the news. "Discover U.S. Spending Monitor" takes a daily poll of spending trends. The U.S. Bureau of Labor releases the *Consumer Price Index* reflecting the expenditures of about 87 percent of the total U.S. population. It is good news for the United States when it is up and bad news when the figure is down. Consumerism is not only newsworthy; it has become integral to American society. Conspicuous consumerism has become the most obvious illustration of American hedonism.

Insight into American hedonism can be found in *Shiny Objects: Why We Spend Money We Don't Have in Search of Happiness We Can't Buy*, written by Baylor University professor of marketing, James Roberts. "Shiny objects" is the phrase Roberts uses to describe the things we want but don't need. "Shiny objects" are the things that many people covet for status and social power, and that many people overspend to acquire.

When people buy for status, the bar always rises. A status-driven consumer can never have enough, even though (as research has shown) buying more doesn't raise happiness. This constant desire for something new and better is called the "treadmill of consumption." This treadmill, as Roberts puts it, is the "process of moving ahead materially without any real gain in satisfaction." Like a drug addict, he says, more and more "doses" of shiny objects are needed to get the same "high." But "acquiring more possessions doesn't take us any closer to happiness; it just speeds up the treadmill."

"Many a man thinks he is buying pleasure, when he is really selling himself to it."

Benjamin Franklin

Of course, buying shiny objects makes the economy grow. Our economy needs consumers to keep on buying and buying. Economist and marketing specialist Victor Lebow put it this way. "Our enormously productive economy demands that we make consumption our way of life, that we convert the buying and use of goods into rituals, that we seek our spiritual satisfactions, our ego satisfactions, in consumption." The pursuit of happiness has become the pursuit of consumption. Lebow suggests that the very meaning and significance of our lives are expressed in terms of consumption.

Many subtle devices make it easy to overspend. The easy availability of "plastic" is one. I'm as guilty as the next person, thinking of my credit card as somehow different from cash. Paying with a credit card puts the pain of paying off into the future, and the future, everyone knows, is uncertain. How we pay affects what we purchase, according to Roberts. Think about that for a minute: how we pay influences our behavior as consumers. Paying with cash or check is painful because we feel the cost of a purchase immediately. Credit cards sit at the other end of the pain scale.

"I'm not so sure you can blame it all on the plastic. Maybe it's the plastic plus lack of good financial education for the vast majority of kids. Getting the monthly statement sure makes the money spent with plastic seem real!"

Posted by Sarah R. on OurValues.org, December 2, 2011.

As Roberts said to me in an email,

"Credit cards greatly minimize the pain of paying, making it considerably more likely that we will buy something. Why is this? First, as humans we tend to discount future events. Making a payment on the credit card in 30 days is seen as no big deal at the time. Second, with credit cards, we aren't required to write down the amount of the purchase (unlike cash which must be counted or checks). We call this a "lack of rehearsal." Both of these aspects of credit card use lead us to over-estimate the amount of money we have available which leads to a greater likelihood of spending what we don't have."

- What "shiny objects" tempt you?

- When have you overspent with your credit card?

- Do you think of credit cards as "cash" or more like a "loan"?

Food and Happiness

Eating is pleasurable, but sometimes we eat to feel happy. The temptation to link eating and happiness is cultivated by tons of advertising and marketing.

Consider the invention and promotion of supersize soft drinks, the size of beverage that New York City Mayor Michael Bloomberg hoped to ban. Bloomberg pushed a proposal to ban the sale of sugared beverages bigger than 16 fluid ounces in the Big Apple. The ban would apply to restaurants, fast food joints, street carts, sports stadiums, movie theatres, delis and more. He agrees with health experts that the consumption of sugared beverages is a major cause of the obesity epidemic.

Everyone has an opinion on this question: Is it your right as an American to buy and drink a sugar-sweetened beverage of any size? If we ban supersize drinks, are we on the slippery slope to socialism? Or, is a ban on big beverages the best thing to do for public health?

The proposed ban isn't going down well with the American soft-drink industry. The industry is fighting back, defending our freedom of choice. One weapon is New Yorkers for Beverage Choices, which defines itself as "a coalition of citizens, businesses, and community organizations who believe that consumers have the right to purchase beverages in whatever size they choose." Their tag line—"What's next?"—is an ominous warning of the slippery slope ahead.

> "If it's legal for food and beverage companies to propagate their products, leaving Americans to think their lives will be happier or more successful if they feed themselves and their children 4.5x and 7x (respectively) the amount of sugar recommended daily (that's a statistical average, with some eating more), why should it be illegal for someone to take a stand against them?"
>
> **Posted by Stephanie Fenton on OurValues.org, July 3, 2012.**

How much choice do we really have when it comes to food and drink? Less than you might think, according to research by food psychologist Brian Wansink. The title of his book says it all: *Mindless Eating, Why We Eat More Than We Think*.

Among Wansink's many studies, perhaps his most famous is the bottomless soup bowl. In this experiment, a participant is invited to eat a bowl of, say, tomato soup. Unbeknownst to the participant, there's a hidden tube connected to the bottom of the bowl that leads to a pump and vat of soup. As the person eats and the level of soup slowly falls, additional soup is slowly pumped in so that the level in the bowl never falls below half. The result? The average person eats 73 percent more soup than they would have otherwise. The reason is that visual cues trump the feeling in one's stomach. If the bowl isn't empty, then you must still be hungry.

> *"Recent studies have also found that over the past 30 years, we've consumed an average of 150 to 300 more calories per day than we used to—50 percent of which come from beverages. Sometimes, we need more than 'Be Healthy, America!' initiatives; we need someone to put a foot down and force Americans to realize what they're really doing to themselves."*
>
> **Posted by Stephanie Fenton on OurValues.org, July 3, 2012.**

Deciding how much to eat or drink isn't always a rational process. Among his other findings, Wansink found that the bigger the group you eat with, the more you eat. The bigger the serving, the more you eat. The bigger the plate, the more you eat. And, the more distractions (like watching TV), the more you eat. Americans use some of the biggest plates and cups in the world. A "large" in Asia is tiny compared to the American LARGE.

- Would you support a ban on supersize soft drinks in your community? Why or why not?

- Do such bans trample your individual freedoms?

- Do you buy the "slippery slope" argument? Why or why not?

Marketing and Advertising

People fall in love with consumer brands. Awareness of "brands" begins early in childhood. Vast sums are spent marketing to children and youth in the United States. The Federal Trade Commission (FTC) estimated that, in 2006, the food and beverage industry spent almost $2 billion marketing to kids, of which $474 million was devoted to promoting the sale and consumption of sugared beverages.

> *"After a day of skiing at Park City Mountain Resort, I heard a 4 yr. old stridently demanding; "I NEED a Starbucks!" My face must have registered my disbelief. Her mother apologetically explained, 'We don't give her coffee, she wants a hot chocolate.' The free hot chocolate served at the Ski School wasn't sufficient?"*
>
> **Posted by W.B. on OurValues.org, October 8, 2012.**

The American Marketing Association defines branding as a "name, term, sign, symbol or design, or a combination intended to identify the goods and services of one seller and to differentiate them from those of other sellers." The object of branding is for consumers to see a particular business or product as the ONLY one that provides what they desire. Some have suggested that through effective marketing, companies are turning America's kids into sales agents. Advertisers expect children to pester Mom and Dad to buy a particular brand. The four-year-old skier "NEEDING a Starbucks" is a prime example (above).

Marketing to children is harmful, according to The American Academy of Pediatrics. Both The American Academy of Pediatrics and The American Psychological Association confirm that children under 10 cannot tell the differences between a commercial and a program. Young kids can't critically comprehend the accuracy or bias of advertising. Marketing to our children makes them extremely vulnerable.

Fighting advertising to kids in the United States has proven to be difficult. Organizations that work to regulate marketing aimed at children and youth are met by an industry that fights back tooth and nail. The advertising industry argues for self-regulation, freedom and choice, while our children remain a captive audience, viewing an estimated 30,000 commercials a year.

> *"Our society does drive multiple messages through multiple mediums whether it's through the bombardment of advertising, social media, the movies etc. that emphasize glitz, glamour, beauty, and overabundance and hedonism. The Kardashians, Jersey Shore and got'ta have more ... of this and more of that, etc. etc. etc."*
>
> **Posted by Rick on OurValues.org, July 2, 2012.**

What's at stake? James McNeal, a kid marketing consultant and author of *Kids as Consumers: A Handbook of Marketing to Children,* reveals the answer: $1.12 trillion. That's the amount that kids influenced last year in overall family spending. "Up to age 16, kids are determining most expenditures in the household," McNeal says. "This is very attractive to marketers."

- Do you think marketing to kids is harmful, beneficial or neutral?

- Have your kids ever talked you into buying something?

- Would you like advertising to kids to be banned like it is in Sweden?

The Prosperity Gospel

Does God want you to flourish financially? He does, says the "Prosperity Gospel" movement. This gospel "preaches that an authentic religious belief and behavior, usually in the form of tithes and other monetary donations, will result in material prosperity," writes James Roberts in *Shiny Objects.* "Conversely, the gospel contends that financial prosperity and success in your private and professional lives is evidence of God's favor."

At first, this sounds like a remake of the Protestant Ethic: worldly success is a sign of salvation. But the Prosperity Gospel is talking about much, much more. The Prosperity Gospel promises that donating money to the church will result in financial success far above the amounts donated. Conspicuous consumption is also a part of the equation, and the clergy who preach the Prosperity Gospel, often leaders of mega-churches, tend to live large.

"The Prosperity Gospel is on the same track as the lottery. Both prey on the gullible and both get more prayers than they should. However, PG is worse in that it preys upon those who are looking for faith guidance."

Posted by The Rev on OurValues.org, December 2, 2011.

How common is faith in the Prosperity Gospel? More than 60 percent of Christians agree that "God wants people to be financially prosperous," according to a *Time Magazine* survey Roberts cites. By the late 1980s, one famous wave of prosperity preachers, including James Bakker and Jimmy Swaggart, was largely discredited. But this style of preaching is so popular that many others have taken up the doctrine. The most popular prosperity preacher today is the best-selling author and TV personality Joel Osteen, who also runs his own huge church in Houston.

TV personality preachers are not the only ones who adhere to the Prosperity Gospel. In 2012, Mitt Romney was the first member of the Church of Latter-day Saints to run for president on a major political party's ticket. His candidacy spurred interest in Mormon beliefs and theology. The Salt Lake Tribune ran an article titled "The Money behind the Mormon Message" shortly after the LDS Church built a $2 billion mall in downtown Salt Lake opposite the iconic Salt Lake Mormon Temple. LDS leadership stated that the church-owned mall would "spread its message, increase economic self-reliance and build God's kingdom on Earth."

> *"The Bible does say that it's harder for a rich man to enter the Kingdom of God than a camel to enter the eye of a needle! People who live far above their means are not honoring God's principles—instead they worship money as a false idol. How can one who truly worships God live in extreme excess when they know that over three billion people in this world—all of whom are God's children—are living in poverty."*
>
> **Posted on OurValues.org by unattributed.**

The Prosperity Gospel is a popular message that isn't going away. But here's the problem. Faith in the Prosperity Gospel can easily lead to overspending, bolstered by the belief that wealth is sure to come. It may also have been a cause of the collapse of the subprime mortgage market, according to a study by Jonathan Walton, a professor of religion. As Roberts notes, many Prosperity Gospel adherents believed that God caused lenders to overlook their poor credit, bad debts and insufficient income, making them fair game for unscrupulous lending practices.

- What's your opinion of the Prosperity Gospel?

- How does the Prosperity Gospel impact our consumer culture?

- Do religious beliefs or philosophies shape your spending patterns?

Fireworks!

One Fourth of July, I bought $100 worth of "really good" fireworks for me and my son. Fireworks in Michigan were "really good" that year, due to a change in the law that allowed the sale and use of fireworks that leave the ground: bottle rockets, skyrockets, reloadable shell devices and the like.

Advocates of the new law said it would help the local economy. Opponents were dubious and worried about the escalation of injuries.

"Are our kids spoiled? To ridiculous levels and it will not end well for the kids or parents, but I'm from a generation that had to make our own fun."

Posted by Davefossil on OurValues.org, July 2, 2012.

But I want to ask a different question: Am I spoiling my child by spending $100 on fireworks—just to make him happy?

I took an empirical approach to the issue: I asked my son if American children were spoiled. Oh, yes, he said, they are. I asked him if he was spoiled. Yes, again. Then I asked if that was good or bad. "Good," he said, "because you get stuff. Bad, because you don't learn how to do things for yourself." Too late to return our fireworks!

His reaction had me thinking: Are we raising a generation of hedonists? "With the exception of the imperial offspring of the Ming dynasty and the dauphins of pre-Revolutionary France, contemporary American kids may represent the most indulged young people in the history of the world," writes Elizabeth Kolbert in *The New Yorker*. Her essay—"Spoiled Rotten"—is a review of several books on the subject. "It's not just that they've been given unprecedented amounts of stuff—clothes, toys, cameras, skis, computers, televisions, cell phones, PlayStations, iPods … They've also been granted unprecedented authority."

"Yes I do think most American kids are spoiled in the sense described in The New Yorker article, which I've read. We tried hard not to spoil our daughters, now 27 and 29, but gave up on enforcing the chores we'd wanted them to do. As the author pointed out, we found it easier to do the chores ourselves than constantly nag and/or argue with them. We are not hedonists. We did not shower them with gifts, privileges were earned, and house rules enforced."

Posted by Athena on OurValues.org, July 2, 2012.

I fretted that my purchase of fireworks was an overindulgence that might be spoiling my son. I found some solace in the advice offered by a reader of my blog: "Have fun, invite the neighbors, and be safe." That's what we did.

- What do you see as evidence that American kids are the most indulged in the world?

- Have we reinforced hedonism as a core value?

- What values about consumption and happiness should we teach the next generation?

What Leads to True Happiness?

We've discussed some of the false paths to happiness. Does this mean the pursuit of happiness is doomed from the start?

It doesn't. We know from Chapter 7 that more money does translate into more happiness, and that there's no upper bound on the effect. But money isn't everything. Psychologists have learned a lot over the years about the causes of true happiness. Three main factors determine happiness: life circumstances, genetically programmed set points and intentional activities. Surprisingly, only 10 percent of a person's happiness can be explained by circumstances—wealth, health, marital status, age, place of residence and so on. About half is due to set points—the built-in dispositions that result from genes inherited from parents. One's set point could be high, low, or somewhere between, but it doesn't change over time. However, 40 percent of your happiness is under your control, determined by your choices, activities, and behaviors.

"Happiness is not best achieved by those who seek it directly."

Bertrand Russell

Happiness researchers have written excellent books about how to increase happiness, such as *The How of Happiness: A Scientific Approach to Getting the Life You Want* by Sonja Lyubomirsky and *Happiness: Unlocking the Mysteries of Psychological Wealth* by the father-son team of Ed Diener and Robert Biswas-Diener. Instead of summarizing their prescriptions for happiness, however, I will point out some of the connections between their recommendations and Core American Values. As you will see, making choices and behaving in ways that are consistent with core values sometimes elevates the experience of happiness and sometimes lowers it.

We know from Chapter 7 that more money can improve happiness and life satisfaction—up to a certain point. In other words, getting ahead is a way to increase happiness, as long as it's not pursued to the extreme. Social comparison—comparing your success to others—is part of the definition of what it means to get ahead. Getting ahead is relative. But avoiding social comparison is a happiness prescription. If you are envious of others' successes or revel in their disappointments, then you cannot be happy.

Living the core value of respect for others leads to greater happiness. Respect for others means esteem and appreciation for all people, regardless of differences in faith, race, ethnicity, sexual orientation or other considerations (see Chapter 1). When we live this core value, we are kind, generous, compassionate, appreciative, and giving to others. We nurture relationships and invest in them. Practicing kindness and nurturing relationships elevate happiness.

> *"The centrality of social connections to our health and wellbeing cannot be overstressed."*
>
> **Sonja Lyubomirsky,** *The How of Happiness.*

The core value of self-reliance can be an obstacle to true happiness. Self-reliance means depending on one's own capabilities, resources, judgment, and wisdom (see Chapter 5). Taken to the extreme, self-reliance translates into social isolation. Avoiding meaningful relationships is a prescription for unhappiness.

Happiness also ensues from the pursuit of a higher purpose, of living a meaningful life. Meaning and purpose come from many sources and can take many forms. The core value of patriotism is one of them (Chapters 2 and 10). That's why George Orwell said there is a spiritual need for patriotism—we have a desire to feel like we are a part of something good, big and immortal.

> *"Don't aim at success. The more you aim at it and make it a target, the more you are going to miss it. For success, like happiness, cannot be pursued; it must ensue, and it only does so as the unintended side effect of one's personal dedication to a cause greater than oneself or as the by-product of one's surrender to a person other than oneself."*
>
> **Viktor E. Frankl,** *Man's Search for Meaning*

- What are your prescriptions for true happiness?

- What are your greatest sources of happiness?

- What gets in the way of your pursuit of happiness?

Summarizing Pursuit of Happiness

This chapter focused on America's passionate pursuit of happiness. Enshrined in the Declaration of Independence as one of our inalienable rights, the pursuit of happiness has propelled Americans in many directions. Not all directions have yielded happiness, which is why America is not the happiest place on earth.

Money can buy happiness, but only up to a point. Sometimes we pursue happiness by buying things—the attractive "shiny objects" that we really don't need and don't produce happiness. Sometimes we overeat. Our children are especially vulnerable to the onslaught of advertising and marketing directed towards them, turning them into lifelong consumers of shiny objects. But it's also true that we spoil our children in an effort to make them happy.

Religion can be a factor. Certain interpretations of Christianity referred to as the Prosperity Gospel support our habits of spending and indulging.

But happiness is not a doomed pursuit. There are many false paths, but happiness researchers have discovered a set of practices that lead to true happiness, such as avoiding social comparisons (evaluating one's success relative to others), investing in relationships, living a meaningful life and being connected to a higher purpose.

Online resources to explore the topic of the pursuit of happiness are available at UnitedAmericaBook.com and include materials for group activities and online reader discussions.

CHAPTER 9

Justice and Fairness

"JUSTICE FOR ALL"—
THE final words of the
Pledge of Allegiance—
reflect the value of justice
and fairness. This is the
principle that all people
should live in harmony
and be treated justly. It is
a Core American Value.

---

*"Justice, sir, is the great interest of man on earth. It
is the ligament which holds civilized beings and
civilized nations together."*

Daniel Webster

Justice and fairness is expressed in many ways. After defining this value, we examine how it shapes the way we think and

what we do. We consider new evidence that humans may be hardwired for justice, and the ways in which justice and fairness play out in tax policies, caring for the needy, the kindness of strangers and America's role in the world.

"If you want peace, work for justice."

Henry Louis Mencken

Defining Justice and Fairness

What does "justice and fairness" mean? In the context of this chapter, justice means fair treatment. Think of the statue of Lady Justice that adorns many courtrooms and courthouses. She is blindfolded to represent impartiality. This means that the rule of law applies equally to everyone; no one is above the law, and decisions are made fairly. Fairness applies to the procedures used to determine outcomes, as well as to the outcomes themselves.

"… the most elementary of moral principles is that of universality, that is, if something's right for me, it's right for you; if it's wrong for you, it's wrong for me. Any moral code that is even worth looking at has that at its core somehow."

Noam Chomsky

Harmony is "a consistent, orderly, or pleasing arrangement of parts," according to Dictionary.com. Music can be harmonious, and so can human relations. Social harmony refers to peaceful relations among diverse peoples and groups. It can range from peaceful coexistence to active engagement characterized by mutual understanding and mutual benefit. The core value of respect for others (Chapter 1) is an integral part of social harmony.

> *"Justice cannot be for one side alone, but must be for both."*
>
> **Eleanor Roosevelt**

In the United States, fairness focuses on protecting the individual. As we saw in Chapter 5, individualism is a Core American Value. Fairness with an extreme focus on individual rights can lead to disharmonious relations. In the non-Western world, fairness is less about individual rights and more about protecting families, community, tribe and nation, as anthropologist Richard Shweder and psychologist Jonathan Haidt have observed.

The goals of fairness and harmony can never be fully realized. American history is chockfull of cases of gross unfairness, injustice, violence and inhumanity. Yet, the core value of justice and fairness remains a high ideal that many Americans strive to live up to.

- What does justice mean to you?

- Does your definition emphasize protecting individual rights? Why or why not?

- How important is social harmony?

Are Fairness and Harmony Important to You?

A *Time Magazine* reporter contacted me about my research on fairness. During the 2012 election season, Republicans and Democrats offered different visions of what fairness means and *Time* wanted to sort it out. What do Americans think about fairness? Do they agree or disagree on what fairness means? Does our country still place a high priority on fairness? In other words, does Lady Justice still wear a blindfold? To respond to the request I turned to my national surveys on values, and the results were striking!

> *"In our hearts and in our laws, we must treat all our people with fairness and dignity, regardless of their race, religion, gender or sexual orientation."*
> **Bill Clinton**

I asked two questions about justice and fairness in these surveys. Here's the first: Do you believe that all people should be treated justly and fairly—even those you don't know? If you do, then you're like most Americans. Just about every American (98 percent) subscribes to this fundamental value. And, there is no difference by political ideology: liberals and conservatives equally endorse this value.

Here's the second: Do you believe that the entire world's people should live in harmony? Think carefully. The entire world includes diverse cultures, religions, languages and lifestyles. Yet the answer to this question is another area of broad and deep consensus among Americans. More than 90 percent of Americans believe that everyone in the world should live in harmony. There's hardly any difference at all between liberals and conservatives.

> *"I believe in this fairness and, yes, it's worldwide."*
> **Posted by Davefossil on OurValues.org, October 15, 2012.**

Now, you might ask, how could anyone disagree with those statements? How could anyone think differently? In other parts of the world, people do disagree with these statements. They don't believe everyone should be treated fairly, or that everyone should live in harmony. And, through much of human history, justice for all was not the ideal. Fair treatment was reserved for one's kinfolk and tribe. All others were fair game for exploitation and mistreatment. If that's hard to believe, then it's because you have so strongly internalized the core values of our society that they seem natural and self-evident. Of course, today disagreements arise when we try to figure out how to treat everyone justly and fairly—but almost all Americans endorse the ideal of fair treatment.

"Fairness is what justice really is."

Potter Stewart

Global studies of character strengths also document the importance of the principle of fairness. As noted in Chapter 1, America is unique among fifty-four nations in placing kindness at the very top of a list of twenty-four character strengths. Fairness is America's second most important character strength. But Americans are not alone in their emphasis on fairness. Other nations in the fifty-four-nation survey gave fairness the No. 1 or No. 2 spot, such as Canada, United Kingdom, Australia, New Zealand, Germany, Belgium, Hungary and Mexico.

- In your daily life, do you try to treat everyone fairly?

- What is your reaction when you see someone being treated unfairly?

- Is the vision of the entire world's people living in harmony just "pie in the sky"?

Are We Hardwired for Justice?

"It's not fair!" What parent is not familiar with this exclamation? Like children everywhere, American children grasp and absorb the concept of fairness early in their development. Different cultures emphasize different aspects of fairness, but every culture has some notion of fairness.

Could it be that humans are hardwired for justice?

It appears to be so, according to a team of brain scientists from Vanderbilt University who published their results in the journal *Neuron*. The team put volunteers in an MRI tube, one by one, and mapped their brain activity as they determined the appropriate punishment for various crimes. These crimes ranged in severity from petty theft to rape and murder. Each one was described in a written scenario. The participants used a scale of 0 (no punishment) to 9 (life imprisonment or execution) to indicate the punishment that fit each crime.

The scientists identified several different areas of the brain that "lit up" when participants were contemplating a crime and deciding on punishment. These regions are associated with the emotions. Here's the key point: More brain activity corresponded with tougher sentences. The scientists caution against over-interpreting their results, but it seems that humans are hardwired for justice and our emotions play a role.

- Do you think we are hardwired for justice?

- What does fairness look like in your family?

- How do you teach fairness to children?

Tax Fairness

President Obama made economic fairness a priority in his 2012 State of the Union Address. What some now call "Obama's fairness doctrine" attracted both support and derision. Fairness was the central theme of the Occupy Movement that began in September 2011 and spread, according to some estimates, to almost 3,000 communities. The movement focused on economic unfairness, especially the widening wealth gap.

"Justice denied anywhere diminishes justice everywhere."

Martin Luther King Jr.

When Obama emphasized "tax fairness" and cited the "Buffett Rule," that those making over a million dollars a year should be taxed more heavily, he was talking about equality of outcomes. Of course, he was far from advocating that everyone should be equal with respect to income and wealth. Rather, he was arguing that the rich should pay more taxes than they currently do, going back to the way things were before the Bush-era tax cuts. His argument was that it was unfair that the rich didn't shoulder a bigger tax burden or at least be taxed at the same rates as the middle class.

> *"Unless the common good is pursued, the gap between the haves and have-nots will only widen. That sets the stage for not only the huge social dislocations of the present, but for revolution in the future."*
>
> **Posted by James Truxell on OurValues.org, October 17, 2012.**

Mitt Romney's vision of fairness focused on equality of opportunity. For example, in April 2012 he said, "We will stop the unfairness of urban children being denied access to the good schools of their choice; we will stop the unfairness of politicians giving taxpayer money to their friends' businesses; we will stop the unfairness of requiring union workers to contribute to politicians not of their choosing; we will stop the unfairness of government workers getting better pay and benefits than the taxpayers they serve; and we will stop the unfairness of one generation passing larger and larger debts on to the next." Increasing taxes on the rich was not part of his plan.

> *"The position that we should also pursue the common good by a redistribution of the nation's assets is currently reviled by many on the right who throw muddy slogans at it such as 'Marxist-tinged' and 'socialist.' Gosh. If they want to throw mud, why not just call it 'Christian'? Someone ... Jesus I think ... once said, 'From everyone to whom much has been given, much will be required; and from the one to whom much has been entrusted, even more will be demanded.'"*
>
> **Posted by James Truxell on OurValues.org, October 17, 2012.**

Do Americans support or oppose the Buffett Rule? This rule would mandate that a household with an annual income of $1 million or more would have at least a 30 percent tax rate. In 2012, Gallup asked Americans how they felt about the rule. Sixty percent said they favor it. Just over a third (37 percent) said they opposed it. Three percent didn't have an opinion.

Sixty percent is a clear majority, but there is a sharp political divide. Three-quarters of Democrats (74 percent) favor the Buffett Rule, but 54 percent of Republicans oppose it. A majority of Independents (63 percent) are in favor. (See Chapter 6 for more on equality of outcomes versus equality of opportunity.)

- How have you experienced the widening gap between rich and poor?"

- Do you support or oppose the Buffett Rule? Why?

- Do you personally feel that the tax rate you pay is fair? Why or why not?

Do We Still Care for the Needy?

My grandfather spent his infancy in an English work-house, along with his mother, consigned there after his father died and mother and child were unable to provide for themselves. English workhouses (also called poorhouses) were the social safety net in England at that time.

Originally, workhouses were for the able-bodied poor who were unable to support themselves on the outside. Life was harsh and unpleasant. Charles Dickens portrayed this tough life in *Oliver Twist*. In the late 1800s, when my grandfather and his mother arrived, the mission had changed, and work-houses were places for the old, the sick, orphans and widows.

"Live so that when your children think of fairness and integrity, they think of you."

H. Jackson Brown Jr.

America had its own version of English workhouses. They were abolished with the creation of Social Security and the widening social safety net. Today, some say we have gone too far, creating a "nanny state"—an overprotective, overbearing, meddling government that treats citizens like children. New York City Mayor Michael Bloomberg was called a nanny-state politician after he proposed to ban supersized soft drinks (see Chapter 8).

Many Americans lament the loss of an earlier time when "we all took care of one another." Is it true that we don't care for the needy as much as we used to?

Actually, the opposite is true. "Earlier generations did at best a mediocre job of caring for the needy," writes social historian Claude Fischer in *Made in America*. In the 1700s and 1800s, he says, you might help out neighbors who were widowed or disabled. You might even adopt a neighbor's orphaned child. "However, the destitute who were strangers, newcomers, or morally suspect instead received directions to leave town." Today, we care more about the needy—even those we don't know—than we did in generations past.

Here's an example. In spring 2009, New Jersey sisters Anna, 9, Grace, 5, and Abigail Buss, 2, learned about hunger and homelessness and decided they should do something about it. The sisters conducted successful independent food drives and started fundraising as well. Together with their parents, they created the "live civilly" initiative. The "Little Man"—a drawing by Grace when she was just two—became their logo.

What does "live civilly" mean? To Anna, it's "being a part of a community—something bigger than yourself." Grace says it's "helping people and doing good things." For Abigail, the youngest, it's "being good."

"We make a living by what we get, but we make a life by what we give."

Winston Churchill

Kahra Buss, the girls' mother, told me that the initiative "is more than just food pantries and feeding people. It is about working together as a group (as a school, as a community, as a state, as a nation) to create healthy individuals, healthy communities. It's about creating a sense of pride and ownership. It is about education and improving the life skills necessary for individuals to grow to that next level. The only way to do that is to fulfill our duty as human beings and to look out for each other … to 'live civilly.'"

The sisters are growing up, and so is their family project. It has become a social movement, formally incorporated in 2011 as "Live Civilly, Inc." and registered as a 501(c)3 non-profit. As of 2013, the organization had raised more than 18,000 pounds of food and provided over 16,000 meals. It had also provided 400 hours of homework assistance and more than 1,000 hours of volunteer assistance—and much more.

> "What do I believe? As an American I believe in generosity, in liberty, in the rights of man. These are social and political faiths that are part of me, as they are, I suppose, part of all of us. Such beliefs are easy to express."
>
> **Adlai E. Stevenson**

- In what ways, if any, are we a "nanny state"?

- How do people in your community care for the needy?

- How do movements like "Live Civilly, Inc." inspire you to help others?

Should Corporations Care for the Needy?

Nonprofits abound that assist those in need. But what about for-profit companies that include humanitarian causes as an integral part of their business? Here's is a unique business model based on the idea that corporations should care for the needy: TOMS Shoes.

TOMS Shoes gives away shoes as fast as it sells them! No, it's not a special sales promotion. This is the full-time business plan at TOMS. Here's how it works. For every purchase of a pair of TOMS shoes, the company gives a pair of new shoes to a child in need. "One for one" is what the company calls it. TOMS—originally called Shoes for Tomorrow—was founded in 2009, and by 2012 had given away more than 1 million pairs of shoes to children in forty different countries.

Blake Mycoskie is "Founder and Chief Shoe Giver" of TOMS. He conceived the idea when he was traveling in Argentina and noticed that so many children went without shoes. Walking is the main mode of transportation in poor countries, posing hazards and limitations for children. With shoes, children can walk farther for food, water and medical assistance. With shoes, their feet are protected from cuts that expose children to dangerous soil-transmitted parasites that can lead to amputation. With shoes, children can attend school. Shoes are often required as part of a child's school uniform but poor families can't afford them.

Since its founding, TOMS has added eyewear to its product line—and it gives the gift of sight to those in need. Whenever a customer buys a pair of TOMS eyewear, the company provides funding "to restore or save the sight of one individual." This funding is used for prescription glasses, sight-saving surgery, or medical treatment.

"Sometimes when we are generous in small, barely detectable ways it can change someone else's life forever."

George Sand

There must be some rare alignment of the stars in southern California. Not only did Blake Mycoskie start TOMS there, another generous shoe-related venture was created around the same time: "Share Our Soles." Share Our Soles—also known as S.O.S.—was founded in 2006 by Greg Woodburn, a sophomore at the University of Southern California. The charity "is dedicated to collecting, and then washing and donating used (but in good condition) running shoes to underprivileged youth in distant nations and local inner-city communities."

Did you catch that "washing" part? This effort has several interesting twists on the TOMS idea of a donation of new shoes connected with each sale. Here, Greg is adding ideas about recycling, charitable giving—and a connection with hard work. Yes, that "washing" is hard work—and it's a value Greg specifically connects with this innovation in generosity.

> *"Sir, I say that justice is truth in action."*
>
> **Benjamin Disraeli**

S.O.S is now "Give Running," a registered nonprofit organization. To date, 15,000 pairs of athletic and running shoes have been given to kids in Los Angeles, Sudan, Uganda, Kenya, Haiti and other places. For many recipients, these are the first shoes they have ever owned—never mind running shoes. Their vision is to give away 50,000 pairs of athletic and running shoes by 2020.

Adversity gave birth to Greg's idea of generosity—a story he tells on the organization's web site. Greg is an avid runner, but in 2006 he was sidelined for months due to injuries. His family taught him that the best way to overcome personal adversity is to help others, he says. "I started thinking about underprivileged kids who couldn't enjoy this great sport—not because of injury, but simply because they couldn't afford running shoes."

With the help of family, friends, and fellow athletes, he surpassed his goal of 100 pairs of running shoes by Christmas 2006, collecting and cleaning over 500 pairs. Shoes are shipped by Sports Gift, a non-profit that donates sports equipment to impoverished kids around the world.

Greg cleaned almost all the running shoes himself. In a story carried by *Reader's Digest*, he says, "People think of it as dirty work. But I like doing it. It's not work I want to pass off on someone else." There's that theme again! Generosity should involve some "dirty work," Greg says. Or, at least, this effort feels better to him because he's active in a hands-on way.

> *"If you can't feed a hundred people, then just feed one."*
>
> **Mother Teresa**

"Helping others overcome their problems has brought me joy and perspective," Greg says. "Joy in hearing from orphanages in Africa that the lives of many kids have been turned from violence and drugs toward school and family simply by reminding them, through a pair of shoes, that they are loved."

So, what do you think of this idea? Greg is unlikely to get nearly as many shoes to needy people as the bigger TOMS effort, but perhaps there are values in Greg's idea that are important as well, even if they're smaller in scale.

- What do you think of TOMS and Give Running?

- How would their mission influence your next purchase of athletic shoes—or what you do with your old pair?

- What similar ideas and programs are you aware of?

The Kindness of Strangers

Reciprocity is a form of fairness. You help me and I help you. This is called direct reciprocity because it involves direct exchange between two people. Indirect reciprocity—better known as "paying it forward"—is also common. Gratitude motivates people to pay it forward—even to a stranger. Here's an example.

"There is no duty more indispensable that that of returning a kindness. All men distrust one forgetful of a benefit."

Cicero

After watching a "60 Minutes" program on organ donation, Anthony DeGiulio decided to donate a kidney and save a life—not a life of someone he knew, but a woman who was a complete stranger: Barbara Asofksy. CBS told the story in a segment on "Medical Miracles."

Barbara's husband had been willing to donate a kidney to her—but he wasn't a match for Barbara. When Anthony stepped in with his donation to Barbara, Barbara's husband was so grateful that he paid the gift forward by donating one of his kidneys to a stranger who needed one.

"Thousands of candles can be lit from a single candle, and the life of the candle will not be shortened. Happiness never decreases by being shared."

Buddha

This pay-it-forward chain continued. The father of a kidney recipient donated his kidney to another stranger. The sister of a kidney recipient donated one of hers to yet another stranger. And so it went, link by link—a life-altering, life-giving chain of generosity. Today, there are many kidney chains, some quite long—and all driven by generosity and gratitude.

"Be an opener of doors for such as come after thee."

Ralph Waldo Emerson

Did you know that there's an app for paying it forward? There's an app for everything, it seems, and the idea of paying it forward hasn't been left out. You can now get a PIF app for your iPhone or Android. It is the official app of the worldwide "Pay it Forward Foundation." This non-profit was founded by Catherine Ryan Hyde, author of the bestselling *Pay it Forward* novel that was made into a film of the same name. Together, the book and film made "pay it forward" part of everyday language and culture.

PIF's mission is to foster the principle itself—"to inspire and educate individuals of all ages and walks of life about the human impact of making a personal decision to change the world through simple acts of kindness—big or small. To help the world reclaim simplicity in a complex world," the foundation's website says.

"Helping people makes you feel good about yourself; it's definitely win-win."

Posted by Sarah Rigg on OurValues.org, August 7, 2012.

- When have you helped a stranger? What motivated you to help?

- When have you received a benefit and paid it forward to a third person?

- What's your most vivid example of the kindness of strangers?

Pay it Forward Continues

The *Pay it Forward* film inspired legions of schoolchildren around the country to create their own pay-it-forward programs. The idea seems to tap into the universal human propensity to help others because we have been helped. It's the fair thing to do.

Once you tune in to the phenomena, you see it everywhere. Have you heard about Detroit's Pay it Forward Initiative? This was founded in 2010 by Charlie Cavell, one of the many young adults who are working to turn around the Motor City. Charlie and his initiative were highlighted by the Detroit Urban Innovation Exchange and National Public Radio. The purpose of the Detroit Urban Innovation Exchange is "to showcase and advance Detroit's growing social innovation movement."

Charlie's Initiative focuses on the problem of joblessness among Detroit's young adults, ages 18 to 25. According to the Exchange article, "Pay it Forward's primary offering is a 16-week internship program. The program places interns in jobs with local partner organizations, such as Quicken Loans and The Salvation Army. During the course of the internship, PIF provides a standard program package of weekly counseling sessions, a transportation stipend, financial management and entrepreneurial classes, as well as wages totaling $2,400. The partner organizations where the interns are placed do not incur any costs."

"One of the rare ways that Christian teaching and secular American thought coincide—it seems that we are called to serve others, not simply to serve ourselves. So the question remains: How should we do that? What are our responsibilities to each other?"

Posted by Greg Garrett on OurValues.org, May 15, 2012.

In a nutshell, the Initiative's mission is to "Employ, Educate, and Empower," as Charlie says in a video interview. "You have to care about your neighbor."

- Can small initiatives like Charlie's "Pay It Forward" really make a difference?

- Do you know of similar initiatives in your part of the world?

- In what ways do you care about your neighbor?

Should America Rule the World?

Just and fairness includes two related ideas—fairness and impartial treatment—as we defined in the beginning of this chapter. We'll end the chapter by considering harmony and controversy about America's role in the world and relations with other nations.

Would the world be a more harmonious place if other countries were more like America? "More like America" means that other countries would be democracies with capitalist economies. For most of American history, says Godfrey Hodgson in *The Myth of American Exceptionalism*, it was thought that this transformation would occur by example. America would be the "city upon a hill" for the entire world to see and emulate. Hodgson is a well-respected British commentator and a keen observer of American life, culture and politics.

"The cause of America is in a great measure the cause of all mankind."

Thomas Paine

In the 20th century, however, the belief emerged that the United States has a special destiny to bring democracy and freedom to the world. After the terror attacks on September 11, 2001, this belief became a military and political program. One result, says Hodgson, is the loss of admiration of America by the rest of the world. "Nothing is more heartily to be wished," he says, "than that the American people should once again see itself, not as a master race whose primacy is owed to the shock and awe inspired by terrifying weaponry, but once again, freely and generously, as first among equals."

Some political leaders believe that America has a moral destiny to remake the world in its own image. What do the American people believe? I wanted to find out, so I asked about it in the same national surveys that identified the Ten Core Values. Here are three statements I include in the surveys. To what extent do you agree or disagree with each one?

- The world would be a better place if people from other countries were more like Americans.
- American values should actively be spread around the world.
- It is America's destiny to set an example for the rest of the world.

Only three of ten Americans (31 percent) agree with the first statement. Almost half (47 percent) disagree with the idea that the world would be a better place if people from other countries were more like Americans. Twenty-two percent are neutral.

We see a similar pattern for the second statement. Just over a third (38 percent) agree that American values should actively be spread around the globe. Forty-two percent disagree, with the remainder (about 20 percent) taking a neutral position.

What about the idea of inspiring change by setting a good example? This remains a strong idea among the American people, regardless of what Hodgson says. Two-thirds of Americans (66 percent) agree that it is America's destiny to set an example for the rest of the world.

- Would the world be a more harmonious place if other countries were more like America?

- Should America lead by example?

- Should America spread democracy by force?

Summarizing Justice and Fairness

Brain scientists believe humans are hardwired for justice, which is one reason why every culture has notions of fairness and justice. But not everyone around the world believes that all people should be treated fairly and live in harmony. However, almost every American endorses this principle. Justice and fairness is expressed in many ways. One is economic justice, and here we examined the issue of tax fairness. We saw that Americans today care for the needy more than generations past did. Even some corporations have incorporated justice into their business models. Finally, we examined America's role in the world and whether American values would make the world a more harmonious place.

CHAPTER 10

Critical Patriotism

"**I LIFT MY** lamp beside the golden door!" This line comes from the sonnet *New Colossus* composed by Emma Lazarus. She wrote it to raise funds for the pedestal of the Statue of Liberty. After her death, the text of her poem was inscribed on a bronze plaque at its base. The *New Colossus* conveys the hope of a nation built on the values of equality, liberty and independence. The poem's words and the Statue of Liberty remind everyone of the nation's high ideals.

Why do Americans love their country? Americans love America for the very values presented in this book. At times, however, the nation doesn't live up to its values. This chapter explores what happens next—how Americans react. After defining critical patriotism, we look at Mark Twain, who was a vocal critic of American foreign policy. We examine the American tendency to criticize and insult elected officials, the paradox that our political institutions are democratic but our workplaces are not, and the role of protests and demonstrations. We take a look at the "too big to fail" policy behind government bailouts of big business, my own personal "protest," and whether public employees should have the right to go on strike.

"I love America. Sometimes I just want to tell it to go to its bedroom and think about what it has done..."

Posted on OurValues.org by unattributed.

Defining Critical Patriotism

Patriotism comes in different flavors. In Chapter 1, we discussed symbolic patriotism—the positive emotions most Americans feel when they see Old Glory or hear *The Star-Spangled Banner*. Critical patriotism is "tough love" of country. It means that when Americans criticize the government or oppose U.S. policies, they do so because they love America and want it to live up to its high ideals. They want to improve the nation. In contrast, uncritical patriotism is "blind love" of country. Think of the catchphrases, "America: Love It or Leave It" or "My country, right or wrong." To the ardent uncritical patriot, critical patriotism is disloyalty—even treason.

> *"My country, right or wrong,' is a thing that no patriot would think of saying except in a desperate case. It is like saying, 'My mother, drunk or sober.'"*
>
> **G.K. Chesterton**

Critical patriotism is a Core American Value, but uncritical patriotism is not. It is true that a majority of Americans say they support U.S. policies simply because they are the country's policies, according to my national surveys, and just under half believe that U.S. policies are morally correct because they are U.S. policies. However, over 90 percent say that, if they oppose some U.S. policies, they do so because they want to improve the nation. And more than three-quarters (78 percent) say that when they criticize the United States, they do so out of love of country. Tough love, not blind love, is the unifying form of patriotism.

> *"Lots of people still want to come to America, so it can't be all bad!"*
>
> **Posted on OurValues.org by unattributed.**

Even when people have different opinions about America, they still agree about core principles. This fact is important to keep in mind when participating in civil discussion with others about our nation. Jefferson, in his first inaugural address (1801), expressed this well when he said, "Every difference of opinion is not a difference of principle."

> "I do love the United States. It is not unconditional love, by any means. Currently, I sense that we have lost our moral compass. We spend too much money on the military and not nearly enough investing in people ... Too many of our own citizens live in dire poverty, go hungry, homeless, and lack access to medical care ... On the plus side, Americans have generally shown themselves to be generous, willing to help their neighbors and creative when presented with difficult challenges."
>
> **Posted on OurValues.org by unattributed.**

- How do you interpret the phrase "Love it or Leave it?"

- What is the role of critical patriotism? Can it go too far?

- On which issues do you voice constructive criticism toward America?

Mark Twain: Critical Patriot?

A few years ago, Hal Holbrook brought his one-man show "Mark Twain Tonight" to Ann Arbor, Michigan. I had high expectations and wasn't disappointed. Holbrook preceded his entrance on stage with a puff of cigar smoke illuminated in the floodlights. Holbrook became Twain that night, giving insight into Twain, the author and the man.

So, when we left the auditorium, I was surprised to hear grumbling from other theatergoers: "Loved Holbrook; hated Twain," one said. "Twain was just so negative. He hated people."

> *"No matter that patriotism is too often the refuge of scoundrels. Dissent, rebellion, and all-around hell-raising remain the true duty of patriots."*
>
> **Barbara Ehrenreich,** The Worst Years of Our Lives: Irreverent Notes from a Decade of Greed.

True, over time Twain became more and more critical of American foreign policies and even of humanity at large. But I think he did so because he had very high aspirations for the nation (and for humanity). He was outraged at the nation's failure to live up to its high ideals. He was a critical patriot, one who criticizes U.S. policies out of love of country and the desire to have it live up to its ideals.

> *"The highest patriotism is not a blind acceptance of official policy, but a love of one's country deep enough to call her to a higher plain."*
>
> **George McGovern**

Twain originally supported American imperialism. He hoped that America could bring democracy and freedom to the Philippines, but soon turned against its annexation when he realized what would actually happen. He felt it was a violation of American ideals. He became an ardent anti-imperialist and a prominent member of the American Anti-Imperialist League. For the remainder of his life, he opposed both American and European imperialism.

> *"People seem to forget that the Government is the people; to not support Government is akin to cutting out our own heart."*
>
> **Posted by kmgeb2000 on OurValues.org, September 12, 2012.**

The War Prayer, published after his death, is a harsh indictment of war, especially the death and destruction wrought on nations by those who conquer them. Depending on the times, it has been viewed as both an unpatriotic story and a patriotic story. "Patriotism is supporting your country all the time," said Twain, "and your government when it deserves it." Twain embraced Critical Patriotism.

"When can the truth ever be considered unpatriotic?"

Posted by kmgeb2000 on OurValues.org, September 15, 2012.

- Who is a "Mark Twain" today?

- Why would people think Twain was unpatriotic?

- When and why would you not support the U.S. government?

Criticizing Elected Officials

QUICK: What's your impression of Vice President Joe Biden? In a single word, what describes your impression of him?

The most frequently used word is "good," according to a 2012 Pew Research Center survey. "Idiot" is the second most frequent. Other negative names include "incompetent" and "clown." Overall, 38 percent of people used negative words to describe Biden, about 23 percent used positive words, and 39 percent used neutral terms.

Is it OK to call our nation's vice president, president or any elected official, by derogatory terms like "idiot"? Of course, it's an exercise of free speech, so it is permissible under that rationale. And, in this situation, the name-calling respondents were hidden behind the survey's cloak of anonymity, so there was no accountability.

> *"All our history has been involved in name-calling and that's not going to change. Our earliest politicians were pretty vile and assaulted each other while in the Senate! This is not news nor is it new. I look down on name callers of all stripes everywhere."*
>
> **Posted by D. Collins on OurValues.org, September 10, 2012.**

But I'm sure some Americans wouldn't hesitate to call Biden an idiot—to his face. And there would be no reprisal for doing so. That's because Americans are free to criticize their government and officials. Many do so not out of malice, but out of love of country and the desire to have elected officials live up to American ideals. This is an expression of critical patriotism or tough love of country.

> *"Regarding name-calling of our elected officials, it appears that anything said is OK. Even understanding free speech completely, our elected officials, no matter what we may think about the person, should be shown respect."*
>
> **Posted by D. Collins on OurValues.org, September 10, 2012.**

What do Americans say, in a single word, about President Obama? "Good" and "trying" are the most frequently cited words. "Failure" and "incompetent" are the most frequently cited negative words. The numbers of Americans who use positive versus negative words to describe Obama are evenly split; there are few who use neutral descriptors.

Candidates Mitt Romney and Paul Ryan didn't escape Pew's one-word test. The most commonly used words for Romney were "honest," "businessman," and "rich" but overall, more negative terms were used than positive. The most frequently used words for Ryan were "conservative," "intelligent," "good," "unknown," "liar" and "young."

The freedom to openly criticize elected officials is something Americans take for granted and many around the world could not imagine. This form of critical patriotism allows everyone to have an opinion and openly express it.

- Would you feel comfortable using derogatory terms for public officials in a public setting? What about in private with family or friends?

- Should there be boundaries for criticizing our government? Why or why not?

- What countries have you visited where critical patriotism is denied?

Critical Patriotism at Work?

How does critical patriotism or tough love play out in the going-to-work, keep-your-job world? Most Americans are familiar with Scott Adams' entertaining Dilbert comic strips. One recurring theme of these comics is derision of the boss. "Upper management" is often portrayed as pompous, ridiculous and out of touch.

What would happen if you openly criticized your boss or those who run the company where you work? What would happen if you attacked corporate policies, even if you did so because you wanted the company to live up to high ideals? Would you fear for your career or safety? Would you get fired, or get a medal?

> *"I found an interesting article discussing the theory of enlightened management on Valve, a video game maker with few rules ... It's even freer than Google's workplace, which actively encourages employees to work on their own projects. Valve, of course, is an extremely successful company. The issue, I think, is that not many companies can get away with this kind of management. Some fields are so traditionally hierarchic that taking that away might damage the companies more than help them."*
>
> **Posted on OurValues.org by unattributed.**

A great irony of American life is that we live in a political system that permits, protects and even encourages critical patriotism, but most Americans work in organizations that are authoritarian in nature. In the extreme, these workplaces are hierarchical with all power at the top. Leaders demand conformity and loyalty. Employees are expected to follow orders, not question them. All of this might be done with a veneer of civility, but workers know the rules: conform, don't question authority, do what you are told.

In other words, the real world isn't like Scott Adams' Dilbert, where employees seem to mouth off at every opportunity. Verbally bashing the boss is such a strong desire that Scott Adams now has opened up a special "Mashups" section on his website where readers can add their own punch lines to the final panel of a comic strip. They're funny, but in a real-world company with jobs so scarce these days I question whether Dilbert would survive.

Of course, things aren't as bad as they used to be. Workers have rights, especially if they are unionized. Laws and regulations exist to protect workers. Enlightened management theories and education encourage much less authoritarianism. In some workplaces, democracy reigns and workers have a big say in what happens, playing a role in decision making, enjoying due process and vocalizing critiques without fear. But these workplaces are rare.

- Are you free to openly criticize the company where you work?

- How is workplace criticism similar to critical patriotism?

- What venues do you have for offering constructive criticism to improve where you work or volunteer?

Critical Patriotism: Protests and Demonstrations

American protests are a longstanding tradition. Protests against the government are a form of critical patriotism. After Hurricane Katrina in 2005, public rage against the Bush administration surged as much as the water spilled over the dikes and dams of New Orleans.

What about the Occupy Wall Street protests? These loosely organized series of protests and demonstrations around the nation in 2011 decried Wall Street institutions and the government's role in bailing out the big banks but failing to reign them in or do something about the widening chasm between rich and poor. Were you sympathetic, opposed, uninterested or perhaps amused?

"Given that my entire family and virtually all of my friends have been deeply harmed by the greed and delusion of Wall Street and the policies that have supported its runaway power, at sixty years of age I find myself dusting my old protest boots off and preparing to head for the street. These young people need to know that at least some of their elders are willing to stand beside them as they speak truth to power."

Posted by Geri Larkin on OurValues.org, October 10, 2011.

The first protests began mid-September, centered on Zuc-cotti Park in the heart of the financial district. Zuccotti Park, once called Liberty Plaza Park, was covered with debris when the Twin Towers were destroyed on 9/11. Seward Johnson's sculpture "Double Check," a lifelike businessman sitting in the park, was dented and covered with ash.

Each day, the Occupy protesters tried to expand their actions, even sparking sympathetic protests in other cities. Wikipedia built a day-by-day timeline.

"I love America more than any other country in this world, and, exactly for this reason, I insist on the right to criticize her perpetually."

James A. Baldwin

If you had a favorable view of the protesters, you were not alone, but you were in the minority. About a third of Amer-icans had a favorable view of the movement, according to a poll taken at that time by Rasmussen Reports. About 41 per-cent held an unfavorable view. One of four didn't have an opinion about the protesters.

Despite lukewarm support for the protesters, a large major-ity of Americans agreed with their basic premise: "Big Banks Got Bailed Out, We Got Left Behind." Rasmussen Reports included this slogan as a question in its survey. They found that 79 percent agreed with it.

> *"I don't give much value to protests of this type or re-call campaigns as I see them as a waste of time and energy. Get out the vote to support candidates that support your values and ideals IS worth the time. All too often these protests don't materialize into any direct political action or voting, hence, they don't mean much in the long run."*
>
> **Posted by Davefossil on OurValues.org, October 10, 2011.**

Wall Street protests expanded across the country and spread to more than 70 cities. The movement drew both fire and acclaim from then-presidential hopefuls and the existing administration. Republicans were much less favorable about the movement than Democrats. Democratic politicians encouraged the protests while Republicans disparaged them. Republican presidential hopefuls were highly critical.

Whatever you thought of the protests, did you think they were authentic? Did the protesters have legitimate concerns, or were they the hapless minions of special interest groups and unions? About 43 percent believed the protestors were expressing authentic concerns, according to the 2011 Rasmussen Reports polls. Thirty-eight percent "believed they were phony efforts drummed up by special interest groups and unions."

> *"I'm trying to be open-minded and listen to what's being said in the media, our politicians, by those on the streets, etc., it's not clear at all. I definitely lean to the opinion that these protesters don't know what they want or what they are doing."*
>
> **Posted by Gorby on OurValues.org, October 13, 2011.**

Whatever your opinion of the Occupy Wall Street Movement, it was a form of critical patriotism. It confirmed our rights of free speech: the right to assemble in public and openly criticize American institutions.

- What did you think of the Occupy Wall Street Movement?

- How did you feel about the protesters? How authentic did you think the protest was?

- Have you ever participated in a public protest? Why?

Too Big to Fail?

What are your feelings about the bailouts of the big Wall Street banks? Do you recall when, in 2008, Lehman Brothers announced its plan to file for protection under the bankruptcy code? Lehman was the fourth-largest investment bank at the time. But the venerable institution couldn't survive the financial firestorm. On September 15, the company fell, making it the biggest bank that the federal government decided NOT to save.

> *"They should have bailed it out. The uncontrolled collapse of Lehman is one of the largest mistakes ever made. It will haunt the U.S. economy for decades to come."*
>
> **Posted by sturle on OurValues.org, September 15, 2012.**

Lehman's collapse may have fueled the deepening financial crisis. Looking back, should the government have bailed out Lehman Brothers along with the other banks and financial institutions? Or, was letting it fail a worthwhile warning that no company was too big to fail?

The federal bailouts of the financial system and the auto industry have received both vociferous opposition and acclaim. The Tea Party was among the most vehement opponents of the big bailouts, along with many other conservatives, who said that Wall Street benefited more than Main Street.

Others, however, said the bailouts prevented the economy from sliding into a deep recession.

Americans continue to debate the wisdom and efficacy of these bailouts. For many, it's an exercise of critical patriotism—criticizing domestic policies because we want the nation to do better and live up to its ideals.

"It's funny—my macroeconomics professor was just giving a lecture about the ups and downs of the economy. He said this is how the economy works (with a hint of sarcasm): if you're a small business and don't make the right financial decisions, you close your doors and go out of business. If you're a big bank, the government bails you out. Why? Because the big banks are so 'important' to the economy that if they go down, the whole economy goes down. Seems logical, but what is it teaching us? If you're one of the biggest, you don't have to worry about consequences? Sounds like that to me."

Posted by Emily T. on OurValues.org, October 10, 2011.

More than seven of ten Americans said that the government should let troubled big banks fall, according to a poll by Rasmussen Reports in May 2012. Only 19 percent said that the government should keep banks in business if they can't meet their obligations. The same poll also found that seven of ten Americans said the government hasn't been diligent enough in pursuing criminal activity on Wall Street.

On the face of it, these poll figures seem to indicate that most Americans think big bailouts are bad ideas and a poor use of taxpayer money. But here's the question I wish Rasmussen Reports had asked as a follow up:

"Should the government let a troubled big bank fail, even if failure meant a 50/50 chance of a deep recession?"

- How do you feel about the bank bailouts?

- What about the auto company bailouts?

- Should the government continue the policy of "too big to fail"?

My Personal 'Protest'

Originally called Decoration Day, Memorial Day means many things to Americans. While working on a series of reflections on the way we treat (and mistreat) our military and veterans, I wrote a story on how my own neighborhood Memorial Day observance disappoints me. These are close-to-the-heart issues for me, because members of my family have fought for our country all the way back to 1812. My father was an infantry sergeant in World War II, his father one of the doughboys of World War I. Our ancestors fought on both sides of the Civil War. I have cousins who are, or have been, in Iraq and Afghanistan.

Here's the story:

My neighborhood's observance of Memorial Day is a small, informal, Mayberry-like affair. I almost expect Sheriff Andy Taylor to make a cameo appearance. It starts with a parade of sorts, somewhat disorganized, led by a few local officials with the obligatory troops of boy scouts and girl scouts, a marching band and hordes of kids on decorated bikes. Along the way, kids scramble for candy tossed by the marchers. The parade winds its way through the streets, ending at a local park. There, we line up along a roped-off corridor to watch an honor guard, listen to the playing of taps, and hear an official read a list of the names and hometowns of Michigan service men and women who died in Iraq and Afghanistan in the past year.

I've never recognized any of the names, though I know where the hometowns are around the state. We feel sad for a few minutes, shaking our heads at the loss and tragedy. Then we eat donuts supplied by the local grocery store, feel better and forget the somber observances. Soon, it will be time for beer and brats in our backyards.

After writing all of these posts on the plight of our veterans, and reading the comments our readers made, I'm feeling now that our little observance of Memorial Day is a sham. I feel hypocritical. We let others fight our nation's battles and neglect the broken and battered veterans who return. We feel we're caring sufficiently for these men and women by inviting our children to decorate their bikes once a year and munch on donuts with our neighbors.

It's not enough. It doesn't feel appropriate to me anymore and, this year, with all that's in my heart and mind I decided not to go.

"Patriotism is not a short and frenzied outburst of emotion but the tranquil and steady dedication of a lifetime."

Adlai Stevenson

But then—and this is the remarkable gift of public forums—Dee, a neighbor who reads my blog, felt moved to post a comment about her compassion for our troops. She had no idea I was one of her neighbors. In her comment, Dee described "our" Memorial Day observance, as well. But, here's what she wrote:

"I'm not sure why veterans are not given the respect that they deserve in our country, but I do know that when I go to our little neighborhood Memorial Day Parade each year, I get very emotional when we honor the veterans. This parade is so hokey and yet so-o-o American. It is truly a neighborhood parade with politicians, Brownies and Cub Scouts, decorated bikes, one fire truck and one police car, and, of course, a handful of veterans. The parade ends up at a neighborhood park where we gather around as names of local enlisted military people are read along with those who have given their life this past year protecting our country. Then a few words are said and taps are played, followed by everyone heading for the donuts!

"What a grand way to teach our children and to remind adults that there are people out there who are doing something to keep our country safe. I feel a deep respect for all who are in the military and greatly appreciate their service. This fun parade on a somber day helps me keep things in perspective."

Wow! You can imagine the conversation this started among friends in our neighborhood! Dee inspired me with her sincere outlook and attitude of appreciation. Next time, I would join the celebration. I might even eat a donut.

Are Public-Sector Strikes Unpatriotic?

It was fall 2012, time to go back to school—but Chicago public school teachers were on strike, exercising their collective right to stop work and protest. It was the first big-city strike since Detroit public school teachers walked off the job in 2006. The Chicago teachers went on strike when contract negotiations fell through. Both sides were pointing fingers.

> *"Unions are important because governments don't know/care or are ineffective at understanding various professions, the risk of that profession to workers, the means they can be unfairly exploited by their managers and the unregulated aspects that simply must be regulated: even if it comes down to the Union to do so at risk of a strike. This is evident in the Teacher's Union and Police and Firefighter unions. These are government services where the workers are so poorly represented, protected, and whose work is so little understood that unions are a necessity. That's a massive failure of governance."*
>
> **Posted on OurValues.org by unattributed.**

Strikes, boycotts and protests are ways in which otherwise powerless individuals can collectively assert power against an organization, company or government. One of the most famous protests in American history was the Boston Tea Party. We look back at this iconic event with fondness and think of protests as quintessentially American. But the actual history of collective actions against those in power has been fraught with difficulty, progress, setbacks—and violence.

A colleague's grandfather was part of the original sit-down strike by the United Auto Workers in 1936 in Flint, Michigan, against General Motors. In a sit-down strike, the workers physically occupy the plant, keeping management and others out. When asked, "Grandpa, what were you striking for?" Grandpa said, "We wanted a fan to vent the fumes." The family still has the baton made out of tires Grandpa used to protect himself. Governor Murphy sent in the U.S. National Guard, not to evict the strikers, but rather to protect them from the police and corporate strikebreakers. The BBC referred to it as "the strike that was heard 'round the world."

Did you know that strikes in the United States have become rare events? Chris Rhomberg, Special Correspondent to CNN, points this out and argues that America would be better off with MORE strikes. In the 1970s, an average of 289 major work stoppages occurred each year, based on Bureau of Labor Statistics data. In the 1990s, the average was only 35 per year. In 2009, there were only five work stoppages.

"I'd say economically, unions do little more than consumers or natural market forces other than threaten the property rights of owners fundamental to our system of exchange. Tragically, but necessary in the eyes of government, when the conflict hits the news the government always sides with owners."

Posted on OurValues.org by unattributed.

What's happened? "We have essentially gone back to a pre-New Deal era of workplace governance," Rhomberg writes. By this he means a return to a period of time in which federal courts denied the rights of workers to organize. This was called the "judicial repression." This changed in 1935 with the National Labor Relations Act, ushering in a long period in which organized labor and business had to reach accords.

Back to the Chicago public school teachers—eventually, they negotiated and accepted a new three-year contract. According to the Chicago Teachers Union, 79.1 percent of its members voted in favor of the new contract. As part of the deal, teachers got a pay raise and agreed to the use of a teacher evaluation system that includes standardized testing for students.

The right for public school teachers (or other public employees, like fire fighters or police) to strike is a rarity. Only eleven states permit it. Since 1968, there have been 827 school teacher strikes, according to data collected by *Mother Jones* magazine. This is a misleading number in one respect: 89 percent of them took place in Pennsylvania.

What is more remarkable is the decline in public-sector strikes. Just as strikes against companies have dwindled to a few, the same trend has occurred for strikes by public employees. Now, it seems, strikes have become un-American.

- What do you think of the statistics regarding the dwindling number of strikes?

- Are strikes unpatriotic?

- Do you support or oppose the right of public employees to strike?

Summarizing Critical Patriotism

Critical patriotism or "tough love" of country is a Core American Value. It is expressed by citizens who criticize the government, participate in protests and strikes, or oppose U.S. policies because they love America and want it to live up to its high ideals. Unlike countries where people are oppressed and persecuted for criticizing the government or official leaders, Americans are free to express their opinions and take action. Sometimes, this sinks to the level of name-calling, but even that is an expression of critical patriotism.

Almost all Americans value the opportunity and freedom to criticize our institutions or oppose U.S, policies, but they often disagree about specific issues. Opinions run the gamut on every issue. Yet, as Thomas Jefferson observed long ago, every disagreement does not indicate a difference of principle. Critical patriotism is one of the ten guiding principles on which almost all Americans agree.

Conclusion: America's Common Ground

EVERY DAY, ANGRY voices decry something in America's changing culture and political movements. They claim that America has lost its way. Collectively, this daily friction erodes our belief that America rests on common ground.

In fact, research shows that Ten Core Values live in the heart of our vast, diverse and complex nation. Americans widely agree on these 10 guiding principles. This truth is empowering because it enables us to rise above the hype of media and politics to see what Americans actually have in common.

The purpose of this book is to document America's core values and to stimulate reflection and respectful discussion about these values, what they mean and the challenges of applying these values.

What do you take away? What are your main insights?

Please go online at UnitedAmericaBook.com and share your thoughts with us and other readers of this book. We value your opinions!

As I reflect on my years of research into the Ten Core Values presented in this book, here are some truths and insights that I hope you found reflected in these pages:

1. A very large majority of Americans endorse Ten Core Values: respect for others, symbolic patriotism, freedom, security, self-reliance, equal opportunity, getting ahead, pursuit of happiness, justice and fairness and critical patriotism. These facts are established with data from national surveys of the American people.

2. The strong endorsement of these core values is shared across differences in age, gender, race, education, income, political ideology, religious faiths and region. These facts also are established with data from national surveys.

3. These 10 values are common ground on which we can build, improve and sustain the nation.

4. The core values balance one another. Together, they form a system of checks and balances. Any single value, taken to the extreme, produces social problems, an unhealthy approach to life and dysfunctional institutions.

5. Americans can disagree sharply about what the core values mean or how to apply them in specific situations or to specific issues. These disagreements do not mean we don't believe in the same fundamental principles.

6. American values are high ideals and many times we don't live up to them. The realities of American society can be at odds with the core values. Failure to achieve these values should not discourage us, but rather motivate us to strive even harder to realize them.

7. American values can be manipulated and misused for political ends. Some politicians attempt to highjack American values, using them to promote their agendas, while in reality their proposals may be the antithesis of these values.

8. Knowledge is power. And, knowledge of our common ground is a potent antidote against messages of disunity, distrust and division peddled by strident voices in media, popular culture and politics. Learning about the core values enables us to resist manipulation and build stronger, more cooperative communities.

There is much to celebrate about being an American. This book offers readers the opportunity to examine, discuss and find ways to build common ground based on these shared values.

If you have been reminded of your own connection with America's core values—then I hope that this book provokes you to action. How will you live these values? Have you discovered new ideas for restarting a civil conversation with people you thought were unreachable? Consider inviting others, especially those who may disagree with you, to read and discuss this book with you.

Become a source of civility yourself. Dare to build common ground. Our challenge is to live up to these core values and to put into practice what we hold most dear.

Acknowledgments

IT TAKES A village to write a book and I'd like to acknowledge members of mine. Many thanks go to David Crumm and John Hile for their visionary leadership in the new world of publishing.

I am grateful to Beth Miller and Megan Walther for thoughtful content editing, to Dmitri Barvinok for copy editing, research assistance and other tasks that take place behind the scenes, and to Henry Passenger for copy editing.

Thanks to Rick Nease for stunning cover art and design.

I am grateful to Brian McLaren for writing the Preface to this book and his nuanced understanding of its message, purpose and importance for civil dialogue in America.

I appreciate all the readers of my blog www.OurValues.org for their participation in our online experiment in civil dialogue and their insightful comments. Many of their comments are reproduced in this book.

My surveys about American Values were made possible through generous support provided by the Carnegie Corporation of New York and the University of Michigan Institute for Social Research (ISR). I gratefully acknowledge the institutional and moral support provided by ISR Director James S. Jackson. The surveys were administered by the staff of the Thompson Reuters/University of Michigan Survey of Consumers and the ISR Survey Research Center. Research and statistical assistance were provided by Phillip Amara, Ashley

Bowers, Wen Chang, Ben Duffey, Esther Lee and Heather Schroeder.

My custom is to save the most important for last: I acknowledge with gratitude and love my wife, Cheryl, for her advice, sound thinking and moral support of this project.

Wayne Baker

About the Author

DR. WAYNE BAKER is Chair of the Management & Organizations area at the University of Michigan Ross School Of Business, Robert P. Thome Professor of Business Administration, and Professor of Management & Organizations. He is also Professor of Sociology at the University of Michigan and Faculty Associate at the Institute for Social Research. Dr. Baker has published over sixty academic articles and five books, including *America's Crisis of Values: Reality and Perception* (Princeton University Press). He blogs five days a week at www.OurValues.org, an online experiment in civil dialogue. Prior to joining the Michigan faculty, he was on the faculty at the University of Chicago. He earned his Ph.D. in sociology from Northwestern University and was a post-doctoral research fellow at Harvard University. Dr. Baker resides in Ann Arbor, Michigan with his wife Cheryl and their son.

Photo Credits

1. Chapter 1, Respect: Photo of "Leona's bumper sticker" provided via Wikimedia Commons by "pbyme."
2. Chapter 2, Symbolic Patriotism: Photo of "Buzz Aldrin and the U.S. Flag on the Moon" by NASA and in public domain.
3. Chapter 3, Freedom: Photo of "Statue of Liberty" provided via Wikimedia Commons by "Francisco Diez" from New York City.
4. Chapter 4, Security: Photo of "Old Glory at Ground Zero" by U.S. Navy photo Journalist 1st Class Preston Keres and in public domain.
5. Chapter 5, Self-reliance and Individualism: Photo of "Ralph Waldo Emerson" provided via Wikimedia Commons and in public domain.
6. Chapter 6, Equal Opportunity: Image of "Ralph Ince in *The Land of Opportunity* (1920) provided via Wikimedia Commons is in public domain.
7. Chapter 7, Getting Ahead: Front cover of "Risen from the Ranks," an 1874 novel by Horatio Alger Jr., the sixth volume in the "Luck and Pluck" series. Now in public domain.
8. Chapter 8, Pursuit of Happiness: Photo of "Snowboarder in Flight" provided via Wikimedia Commons by "Sören from Germany."
9. Chapter 9, Justice and Fairness: Photo of "Golden Lady Justice, Bruges, Belgium," provided via Wikimedia Commons by "Emmanuel Huybrechts from Laval, Canada."

10. Chapter 10, Critical patriotism: Image of "Mark Twain, New Hampshire" provided via Wikimedia Commons and in public domain.
11. Author photo by Cheryl Baker. Reproduced with permission.

Colophon

READ THE SPIRIT Books produces its titles using innovative digital systems that serve the emerging wave of readers who want their books delivered in a wide range of formats—from traditional print to digital readers in many shapes and sizes. This book was produced using this entirely digital process that separates the core content of the book from details of final presentation, a process that increases the flexibility and accessibility of the book's text and images. At the same time, our system ensures a well-designed, easy-to-read experience on all reading platforms, built into the digital data file itself.

David Crumm Media has built a unique production workflow employing a number of XML (Extensible Markup Language) technologies. This workflow allows us to create a single digital "book" data file that can be delivered quickly in all formats from traditionally bound print-on-paper to nearly any digital reader you care to choose, including Amazon Kindle®, Apple iBook®, Barnes and Noble Nook® and other devices that support the ePub and PDF digital book formats.

And due to the efficient "print-on-demand" process we use for printed books, we invite you to visit us online to learn more about opportunities to order quantities of this book with the possibility of personalizing a "group read" for your organization or congregation by putting your organization's logo and name on the cover of the copies you order. You can even add your own introductory pages to this book for your congregation or organization.

During production, we use Adobe InDesign®, <Oxygen/>® XML Editor and Microsoft Word® along with custom tools built in-house.

The print edition is set in Minion Pro and Avenir Next.

Content editing by Beth Miller and Megan Walther.

Cover art and Design by Rick Nease: www.RickNeaseArt.com.

Copyediting by Dmitri Barvinok and Henry Passenger

XML styling, digital encoding and print layout by Dmitri Barvinok and John Hile.

If you enjoyed this book, you may also enjoy

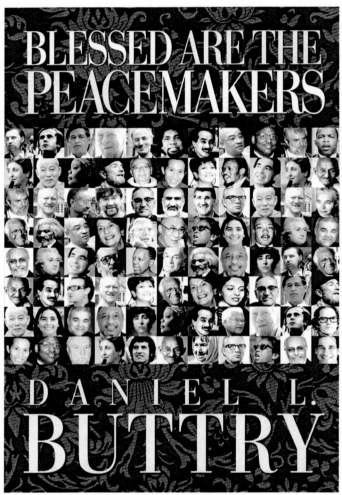

In the pages of this book you will meet more than 100 heroes. Watch out! Reading about their lives may inspire you to step up into their courageous circle.

http://www.BlessedAreThePeacemakers.info

ISBN: 978-1-934879-76-4

If you enjoyed this book, you may also enjoy

THE NEW BULLYING

HOW SOCIAL MEDIA, SOCIAL EXCLUSION, LAWS AND SUICIDE CHANGED BULLYING

The authors show that bullying has changed considerably in recent years, but that some adults are not aware of the change. This book is intended to document that change for anyone who works with youth or simply cares.

http://www.readthespirit.com/bookstore/books/the-new-bullying/

ISBN: 978-1-934879-63-4

If you enjoyed this book, you may also enjoy

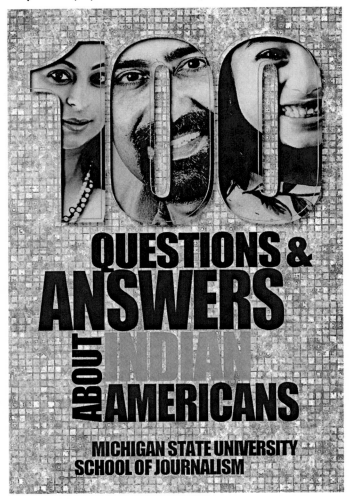

Part of the Michigan State University School of Journalism series in cultural competence, this guide to Indians in America is intended for people in business, schools, places of worship, government, medicine, law enforcement, human resources and journalism.

www.ReadTheSpirit.com/bookstore/books/indian-americans.com

ISBN: 978-1-934879-07-8